My Life in Pictures

The Bodley Hea

by Charles Chaplin

London/Sydney/Toronto

Designed by
Introduction by

Printed

David King
Francis Wyndham

eat Britain

Contents

The Chaplin Image

On giant movie posters and tiny cigarette cards, in
children's comic-books and scholarly studies of the art of the cinema,
the Chaplin image has proliferated over the past sixty
years until it has become deeply embedded in the consciousness of
an international public. This colour section shows some
of the forms it has taken, from an early advertisement depicting him in a
romatic mood (opposite) to his mature artistic triumphs

This early series of cigarette cards which, when completed, relate a fictitious Chaplin adventure, is a typical example of the iconography he inspired

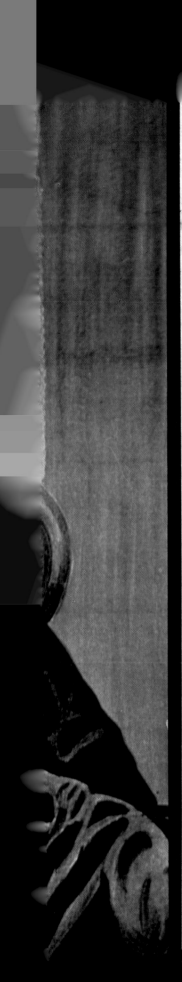

Above: The Chaplin image on a Spanish playing card. At left: a French poster, 'His Night Out'

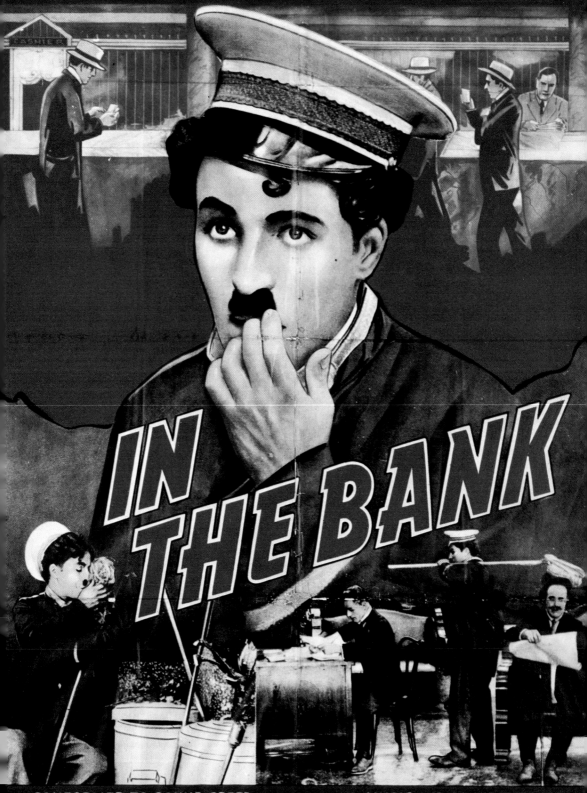

KING OF COMEDY FILM CORP. 698 9TH AVE NEW YORK CITY

Presents

CHARLES CHAPLIN

IN THE BANK

CONFORMED TO SOUND SPEED   MUSIC AND SOUND EFFECTS

Above: a poster for the re-issue of a 1915 two-reeler.   At right: an ingenious cut-out game from a film magazine

MOVY-DOLS

REG. U. S. PAT. OFF, BY PHOTOPLAY MAGAZINE

PUBLISHED BY PERCY REEVES, 1245 S. STATE ST. CHICAGO
ALL RIGHTS PROTECTED

CHARLIE CHAPLIN   No. 4
and some of his most popular Photoplay characters.

First cut out the page so you can handle it conveniently.
Then cut out figures carefully on outlines, with scissors.
Use sharp knife point to cut along dotted lines.
Letters indicate which figures may be used together.

CUT SLIT UNDER NOSE FOR MOUSTACHE

THE LID

THE MOUSTACHE

USE B HEAD

CUT DOTTED LINES

CUT DOTTED LINE

USE HEAD B

EASEL BACK FOR D¹ FIGURE

CHARLIE CHAPLIN. HIMSELF

"CHIP" HIS CO-STAR IN "A DOG'S LIFE"

IN "SHOULDER ARMS"

THE OLD ORIGINAL OUTFIT

USE HEAD B

CUT DOTTED LINE

IN "THE ADVENTURER"

CHARLIE CHAPLIN'S COMIC CAPERS

Chaplin as a comic-book hero in the popular American press

CHARLOT JOUE CARMEN

FANTAISIE EN DEUX EPISODES

1er épisode LE COUP DE FOUDRE

Guy Leymarie

**AGENCE
GÉNÉRALE
CINÉMATOGRAPHIQUE
. PARIS .**

2me épisode SOUVENT FEMME VARIE

ATELIER LEYMARIE 10 RUE SEVESTE . PARIS.

Les aventures acrobatiques de CHARLOT

Charlot contrebandier

xte et dessins de HOMEN

14. SOCIÉTÉ PARISIENNE D'ÉDITION, 43, rue de Dunkerque, PARIS (Xe). - 45 fr.

Les aventures acrobatiques de CHARLOT

CHARLOT AVIATEUR

Texte & dessins de THOMEN

Nº 15. SOCIÉTÉ PARISIENNE D'ÉDITION, 43, rue de Dunkerque, PARIS (Xe) - 4.

Les aventures acrobatiques de CHARLOT

LES EXPLOITS SPORTIFS DE CHARLOT

texte & dessins de THOMEN

SOCIÉTÉ PARISIENNE D'ÉDITION
40 fr. APRÈS BAISSE 36 fr.

Les aventures acrobatiques de CHARLOT

CHARLO ET LE KID

texte & dessins de THOMEN

Nº 7. SOCIÉTÉ PARISIENNE D'ÉDITION, 43, rue de Dunkerque, (PARIS Xe) - 50

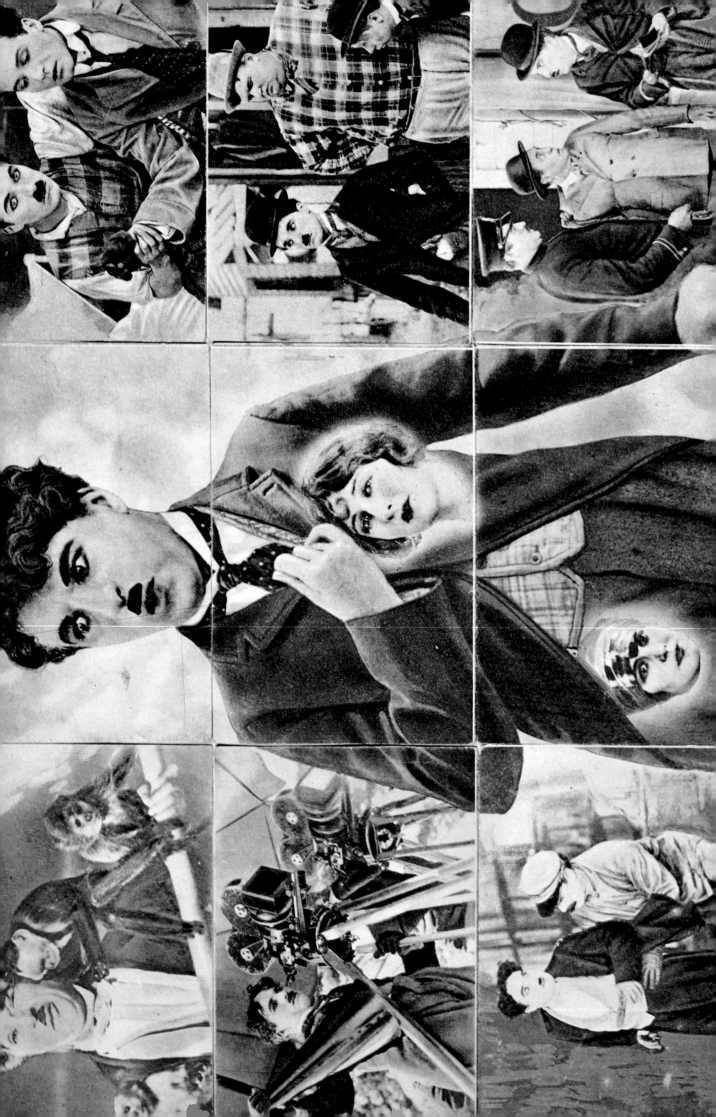

Introduction
by
Francis
Wyndham

It is rare to find the two complementary aspects of art, the creative and the interpretative, united in a single being. Charles Chaplin is doubly a genius – as a performer, and as a maker of films. This synthesis places him beyond comparison with any of his 'rivals' in either sphere. No artist since Charles Dickens has combined the widest popular success with the highest critical acclaim in the way that Chaplin has. If he did not exactly invent the cinema, it may be said that his art and the medium have matured side by side. Every artist is unique: Chaplin is somehow more than this. It is almost impossible to imagine the twentieth century without Chaplin in it. One thinks of him as having been 'necessary' in a sense that would normally only apply to a great scientist, philosopher or mystic – and he has made no pretensions in any of these directions. He is simply an entertainer.

Like the mystery of birth, original art must ultimately defy analysis. Its full effect can only be felt and can never be completely understood or satisfactorily explained. The prime secret will always remain hidden, buried in the intricacies of a human

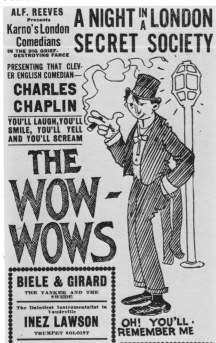

Prophetic poster for the first appearance of Chaplin on the American stage

personality. This book provides visual clues to three elements of that personality: the man, his work, his life. These formative agents interact with each other, shaping, modifying, influencing, and the relationship between them will inevitably sometimes

Chaplin's father and namesake was a popular singer in the English music-halls

seem contradictory.

There is a contradiction at the heart of Chaplin's work, which has always been excitingly ahead of its time while simultaneously expressing a reassuringly old-fashioned quality. Although his great celebrity was achieved as early as 1914 in the most 'modern' of all art forms, the cinema, his performances were essentially the perpetuation of an ancient tradition. Through his apprenticeship in the music-halls (which were themselves then well past their prime) he was able to develop a pantomimic gift which had its origins in the strolling tumblers of the Middle Ages and the classic sophistication of the Commedia dell'

Arte, emerging as master of a comedy technique both simple and refined, where the crudest farce can be interpreted with the purest style.

This accounts for the extraordinary, almost subliminal power of those first flickering appearances, which seized on the world's imagination through means other than words and has never quite relinquished its grasp of it. Charlie Chaplin is more than just famous: his image remains part of our psychic heritage. For members of several generations, it literally recalls their childhood – but its hold goes deeper than that. It seems to belong to some universal, almost abstract concept of childhood, beyond time and space; like certain passages in Dickens, it is as familiar and mysterious as a recurring dream.

The immense popularity which he won through those early, fast, cheap, elementary diversions gave Chaplin a weapon which a less adventurous or a more complacent artist might have used merely to consolidate his success. Instead, he used it to enlarge the horizons of the medium which – almost by accident – had given him the opportunity to realise his talents and to find an audience for them. At first, in the dozen films he made for the Mutual Company under his own total artistic control, he polished the pattern already established by the Keystone and Essanay quickies, and soon perfected it. Then, he widened his scope: such films as *Shoulder Arms*, *The Kid*, *The Pilgrim*, *The Gold Rush* and *The Circus* were innovations in their era to an extent which it is difficult to appreciate today, although it is still easy to enjoy them as dramatic comedies.

But the fact of being 'new' – in the sense of revolutionising technique – has never really been the point of Chaplin's films. He alone dared to go on making silent pictures long after the advent of the talkies – and, of course, he triumphantly got away with it. *City Lights*, which came out in 1931, is perhaps his most perfect film; and *Modern Times*, which followed five years later and in which he still did not speak himself (apart from an inspired wordless song), is among his most inventive and original. Both are timeless classics.

26

WHEN CHARLIE CHAPLIN LIVED IN LONDON.

This Song may be Sung in Public without Fee or Licence. Except at Music Halls

As the Church Bells Chime

Written by
Norton Atkins

Composed by
Felix McGlennon

Sung by
CHARLES CHAPLIN.

Copyright.   Price 4/-

LONDON.
FRANCIS DAY & HUNTER.
142, CHARING CROSS ROAD, OXFORD STREET END.
Smallwood's Celebrated Pianoforte Tutor. Smallwood's 55 Melodious Exercises, etc.

Left (above) Charles Chaplin, the vocalist, father of Charlie Chaplin. Left (below) Charlie Chaplin's headmaster. Centre, "As the church bells chime," a song sung and made popular by Charlie's father. Right (above) Spencer Chaplin, Charlie's grandfather. Right (below) George Jackley, the comedian, old friend of Charlie.
[Exclusive "Daily News" photographs.

A newspaper celebrates the triumphant return of Charlie Chaplin to London in 1921

His masterpiece of the 1950s, *Limelight*, boldly exploited such old-fashioned elements as melodrama and sentimentality without a hint of self-consciousness – and is therefore distinguished by an artistic integrity which will ensure its survival long after many 'cleverer' exercises in nostalgia have been forgotten. It is ironic that his last film, *A Countess from Hong Kong* (a minor but by no means a negligible work), was violently attacked for being 'dated'. It appeared (in 1967) when the vogue for making films about other films, for 'camp' and pastiche, was well under way, and when almost any artificial approximation to a Hollywood comedy of the 1930s, heavily signposted by 'in' references, would have been applauded by the so-called *cognoscenti*. There was nothing facile about *A Countess*, however light its tone; it was the real thing at the wrong time. To say that Chaplin 'dates' is as crass as to submit his work to the straitjacket of any fashionable interpretation: Freudian, Marxist, Existentialist or Saussurian. He can no more be 'dated' than he can be 'up-to-date'; like all great artists, he is essentially dateless.

And, like some great artists, he is beyond taste. His comedy began, as it were, in the nursery, where bottoms are considered funny, and never graduated to the genital humour of the barrack-room or the saloon bar. It is cheerfully vulgar rather than slyly prurient – but it is definitely not in 'good taste'. In his *Autobiography* he quotes with pleasure a 'quiet and courteous' Southern gentleman called Judge Henshaw, who tells him: 'What I like about your comedy is your knowledge of fundamentals – you know that the most undignified part of a man's anatomy is his arse, and your comedies prove it. When you kick a portly gentleman there, you strip him of all his dignity.'

A hostile critic, writing in 1919, made a similar point: 'When one of the bewhiskered artists in a Chaplin exhibition picks up a pitchfork and delicately impales another member of the cast in the seat of his trousers, the packed mass in front of the screen chortles and screams and shrieks – and the exchange manager wires the returns to the head office.' The kick in the pants is a timeless gag: it mingles comforting overtones of infantilism with an adolescent satisfaction in witnessing the deflation of authority. For adults, it can easily be tediously repetitive, or unpleasantly suggestive of a covert sadism. When Chaplin uses it, it is funny – and there is really no more to be said.

He can transgress against good taste in other, less obvious ways. The last speech in *The Great Dictator* is

The American tour which led to his first film contract

quite out of key with the rest of the film and may therefore be called an artistic error. The brilliant *Monsieur Verdoux* embarks on philosophical and political subtleties which Chaplin (more interested in emotion and instinct than in the intellect) does not fully explore. Similar imperfections can be found (and have been recognised by Chaplin himself) in several of his other films.

In the long run, they hardly matter at all. He belongs with the great imperfect artists, with Dickens and Balzac rather than with Jane Austen or Flaubert, and he can afford to offend in detail without degrading the effect of the whole.

None the less, his methods of working and his attitude to the result have always been those of a perfec-

tionist – imperious and uncompromising. While he was filming, the whole of his being would be dedicated to the task on hand. Time, money, the feelings of other people – all would take second place. Several of his colleagues have left accounts of this experience, and of how exhausting they found it. For him, inactivity was – and is – a form of torture. 'Any time that I was really stuck for an idea,' he says, 'I would retire to my dressing-room and tell the others: "I have to go into the Gethsemane!" Sometimes I'd be there for days with my chin on my chest, staring at nothing, saying over and over to myself: "There *must* be an answer to this!" The *real* hard work is in thinking, just thinking. For several days I would be in agony – then the word would go round the studio: "Fine! Charlie's got it!" It would probably be a very small idea – but something that could be elaborated while we were doing it until it turned into a good, inventive gag. It doesn't matter how serious the story is – it all amounts to a bit of business or a gag. In the end, everything is a gag.'

When he was making *City Lights* he spent days coaching the inexperienced

A publicity picture from the early Hollywood era, with Buster Keaton extreme right

Members of the Mutual company in 1917. Alf Reeves, Chaplin's manager, on the left; Edna Purviance on Chaplin's right

Virginia Cherrill in the difficult part of the blind flower-seller. 'I would take anybody and make them act!' he boasts. 'I told her: "When you offer the flowers, *bend* your arm, make a nice movement, don't be quite so threatening!" I'm sensitive to line, I'm influenced by movement. It was so hard to get the right effect for the end,

Francis X. Bushman, Chaplin, and G. M. Anderson, also known as Bronco Billy

when she pulls him towards her and delicately feels him and gradually recognises who he is through the tips of her fingers.' After hours of rehearsing, just when it seemed that the scene was right, the actress interrupted work because she had an important appointment with her hairdresser. Chaplin was so furiously upset that he

closed the studio and went to bed for several days in a sulk of frustration. But in the end, he got his effect: the closing moments of *City Lights* made history.

'I love women, but I don't admire them,' says Monsieur Verdoux, the anti-hero of Chaplin's bitterest film. At the time he started to write this script, Chaplin had reason to be disillusioned with the opposite sex. The heroines of his films, like those of Dickens's novels, tend to be young, exquisite, enigmatic and rather blank: symbols of innocence and purity rather than realised individuals. His first, abortive romantic relationship had been with a very young girl, Hetty Kelly, and her delicate but incomplete image seems to recur throughout his creative work – as the dance-hall girl, the circus equestrienne, the flower-seller, the *gamine*. They are objects of distant worship, and if they are capable of giving pain it is only because they are ignorant of their own power to inspire devotion. The guilty mother in *The Kid* and the corrupted courtesan in *A Woman of Paris* belong to a slightly different type – but even they become

reformed characters before their stories end.

Mildred Harris and Lita Grey, Chaplin's first two wives, were both very pretty and very young when he married them. Both disappointed him almost immediately. In the first case, beauty concealed a rather empty character, and in the second it masked

G. M. Anderson, founder of Essanay Co.

Chaplin 'boxing' with Mack Swain, the 'heavy' in seventeen of his early pictures

a mercenary and vindictive nature. His marriage with Paulette Goddard had a firmer foundation, but her personal professional ambition ensured that it could only be comparatively temporary. It is possible that Chaplin has never quite lost a certain sentimental indulgence for the figure of the 'gold-digger', who makes harmless, decorative and diverting appearances in several of his films, but this must have been painfully damaged by the hideous imbroglio with Joan Barry. Because he was rich and famous, Chaplin was an easy victim for any publicity-seeking predator; in spite of being rich and famous, he found himself treated in this case with flagrant injustice by the public and the press. Anger and hurt at the hostility so easily aroused towards him in his adopted country provided a motive force for *Monsieur Verdoux*; and the malevolent, hysterical shade of Joan Barry may be discerned behind its apparent cynicism.

(Perhaps this unpleasant episode in Chaplin's life should be clarified here. After the United States had entered the war, Chaplin made himself unpopular in reactionary circles by speaking in favour of opening a Second Front for Russia. At about this time, a paternity suit was brought against him by Joan Barry. A blood test proved conclusively that he was not the father of her child – but in spite of this a verdict was eventually delivered which made him responsible for a baby that could not be his. This *Alice in Wonderland* situation took a more sinister turn when the Federal Government indicted him under four fantastic counts. Two of these invoked some antiquated law, under which he was said to have interfered with Barry's rights as a citizen by paying her return fare to the East at a time when she was under arrest for vagrancy. The other two accused him of

Early 1916: signing the Mutual contract with John L. Freuler and Sydney Chaplin

violating an obscure piece of legislation called the Mann Act. To quote from his *Autobiography*: 'Every once in a while the Federal Government used this piece of legal blackmail to discredit a political opponent. The original intention of the Mann Act was to prohibit the transporting of women from one state to another for prostitution. After the abolition of the red-light district there was little legitimate use for it, but it is still used to victimise citizens. Should a man accompany his divorced wife over the border to another state, and have intercourse with her, he has committed an offence against the Mann Act and is liable to five years in prison. It was this bogus piece of legal opportunism upon which the United States Government brought an indictment against me.' He was acquitted on all four counts.)

At the height of the Joan Barry scandal, and while he was working on the early stages of *Monsieur Verdoux*, he met Oona O'Neill. She was very pretty and very young and he married her. History, instead of repeating itself in a boringly predictable way, now went into a spectacular reverse. It turned out that Oona's inner nature

Chaplin with Max Linder, the French comedian (at left), in Hollywood in 1917

was of a piece with her outward beauty. She is clever, witty, calm, loyal and totally lacking in self-regard or self-interest. She has made her love for him the centre of her own life, with the result that he soon came to depend on her entirely. Their marriage is perfectly happy. When she comes, rather shyly, into the room, he reaches out a hand to hold hers; he will interrupt

By the time these comic publicity pictures were taken, Chaplin's name was famous all over the world

Charlie Chaplin - Pola Negri

Verlag_Ross, Berlin S W 68

Pola Negri was a German star with whom Chaplin formed an 'exotic relationship'

any conversation to blurt out, unembarrassingly, how much he adores her. He has numerous nicknames for her: 'the old woman', 'the missus', 'the old girl'. If she leaves his side for a moment, he looks distressed until her return. Himself a sensitive, proud, egotistic, touchy man, the essential artist, he marvels at those qualities which make her the ideal artist's wife: tolerance, intuition, selflessness, tact. The only flaw in their domestic harmony – occasional misunderstandings with their children as each in turn ceases to be a child – springs from the very intensity and completeness of their mutual happiness. The delight which Charlie and Oona take in each other's company tends to isolate them in a self-sufficient world of love. This atmosphere is utterly charming for their friends, but its effect on a nearer relationship might be unintentionally exclusive. If Chaplin has failed to achieve a wholly unselfish sympathy with his children, he has triumphantly succeeded in eliminating any dichotomy between 'love' and 'admiration' in his attitude towards the woman in his life.

'I love the public, but I don't admire them,' says Calvero, the hero of *Limelight*, Chaplin's most melancholy film. 'Individuals, yes. As a crowd – a monster without a head.' Politically, Chaplin is a humanist; the 'Communist sympathies', which caused so much fuss in the hysterical atmosphere of America at the start of the Cold War, were sympathies and nothing more. How could so fierce an individualist have ever formed a closer link with a system in which supreme power devolves on the State? To the charge of political naivety, which has been brought against him from both the Left and the Right, he has a dignified reply. 'I am a poet. I am a spiritual anarchist. I am not patriotic. I am amoral. I am an artist.' By these statements, he really means that he is an egalitarian idealist. He wants to be left alone, and to leave others alone: wars, governments, politics belong to a nightmare world he would now rather ignore. He cannot forgive mankind for the Nazi atrocities and for the atom bomb: 'It was the Americans who dropped it.'

As a child, he suffered the humiliation of extreme poverty. More important, he had to watch his beloved mother suffer it too. He triumphantly survived, but she remained a casualty of social injustice until her death. One result of this circumstance (and there were several) was that he became obsessed by money, which he sees in the simplest terms – as a protection from misery, and nothing else. For him, the possession of wealth is not so much a positive good to be enjoyed as a negative advantage – a shield against the lack of it. He knows from direct and bitter experience that poverty – however poetic it may appear from a comfortable distance – is essentially evil and obscene. Chaplin believes that capitalism – based as it is on an assumption of financial inequality – must therefore collapse before long

A French magazine recreated Chaplin's return to his Kennington home in 1921

under the weight of its own self-destructive guilt. He himself does nothing to hasten this collapse, and continues to take a rather grim satisfaction in adding to his personal wealth and that of his family. He sees no reason why a hated system should not be exploited while it still exists – and it's not as though he hasn't earned the money!

Charlie Chaplin lived in this house on Beechwood Drive where he entertained all the celebrities who visited Hollywood throughout the 1920s

A visiting celebrity: Winston Churchill

An early cartoon which foreshadowed his political troubles several years afterwards

This attitude has struck some observers as inconsistent, and possibly even hypocritical. They do not understand that the rich and famous and fulfilled man whom the world sees still considers himself a victim maimed for life by that early catastrophic shock. Children expect the world to be fair, and often never recover from their first brutal discovery that it is nothing of the sort. Poverty is unfair – that is why he hates it. And individuals *en masse* become a crowd, a monster without a head, and a crowd can be unfair too; which is why he loves his public but does not admire them. When, in 1972, he returned to Hollywood after an absence of nearly twenty years, to be honoured by the remnants of a legendary community which he more than anyone had helped to create, there was a crowd to applaud him. 'You are all sweet, wonderful people,' he told them. It is interesting to speculate about the thoughts he left unspoken on that moving and ironic occasion.

Yet a rich man, who has beaten the world at its own game – even if the methods used have always been scrupulously fair – may become a kind of exile from his essential self. As far as I know, Chaplin has never openly expressed this thought, but his increasing absorption in memories of his early life suggests that it may have

occurred to him. The peaceful, private, protected existence in his Swiss retreat is not quite enough for him, however idyllic it may appear to outsiders. He loves to come to London, almost anonymously, and to stay at the Savoy Hotel. Here he can sit in the window of his suite and gaze for hours over the river towards the altered landscape of his Cockney origins. On these visits, his favourite diversion is to hire a car, and, with Oona beside him, to tour those same sad streets from which he was once so eager to escape. They are far less slummy now than he remembers them – and he does not find the change for the better. In old age, Chaplin has lost interest in the achievements of his prime. He is mainly concerned with what he will do next, and with that obscure period of his life before his genius had been given a chance to define itself. The tragedy of those days has acquired a poignant beauty for him with the passage of the busy years. 'I miss the vitality of street life, the colour and the characters. Those lovely little houses, going down in rows, with long gardens behind . . . Now it's all wretched high-rise flats. But some of the pubs still have the same Victorian atmosphere.'

It would be misleading, however, to place too much emphasis on the 'melancholy clown' aspect of Chaplin's personality. Even in old age, he still lives in a world of laughter. When Oona reacts to his jokes as if she were hearing them for the first time, she is not playing the diplomatic wife – she really *is* hearing them for the first time, and they really are funny. When I first met him I knew that he was seventy-five but could hardly believe it. He moved with the agility of a dancer, and the vitality of his responses was both demanding and rewarding for his interlocutor. His manner is confidential, demonstrative, almost coquettish; yet there is always the possibility of impatience, a sudden sternness. There is arrogance in his nature, but not a trace of self-satisfaction. As with all good conversationalists, nothing is taken for granted: any idea is welcome, provided it is not a platitude. He has some of the small vanities often found in very famous people, but this is preferable to inhuman remoteness, of which there is not a sign.

And he is the most enjoyable sort of mimic, whose imitations are spontaneous and lacking in malice. They have nothing about them of the party turn: in conversation a name is mentioned and Chaplin will, almost un-

Charlie Chaplin   George Robey

Charlie Chaplin   George Robey

Another visiting celebrity: with the famous English comedian, George Robey, in 1931

consciously, *become* the character he wishes to suggest, physically as well as vocally. The extraordinary grace of his gestures, combined with the accuracy of his ear, subtly define the ludicrous

essence of a past occasion: Truman Capote using all his tact in persuading Chaplin to delete the word 'cognisant' whenever it appeared in his *Auto-biography*; Elsa Maxwell at a Manhattan party croaking out unpublished Cole Porter to a hushed and reverent audience; Howard Hawks, who disapproves of swearing, nearly abandoning his principles after some ghastly disaster on the set, and finally exclaiming 'Heavens to Betsy!'; Jimmy Walker, flamboyant Mayor of New York, having an undignified row with his Ziegfeld Follies girl friend on the way to a pompous civic reception; Duse upstaging her leading man simply by warming her hands at the fire; a nervous young actor endlessly repeating his single line, 'There's a man downstairs who calls himself Solomon Isaacs,' and giving it so many different interpretations that it eventually loses all meaning; Anna Sten, the Russian film star, wrecking take after take by obstinately demanding 'Vere is the wodka?'; Gus Elen, idol of the music-halls, singing:

'With a pair of opera glasses
You could see to 'Ackney Marshes
If it wasn't for the 'ouses in between.'

Behind the gaiety and romance of Chaplin's personality – and by no means detracting from the glamour of his company – there lies a strong awareness of violence and horror. Certain subjects both repel and fascinate him. Surprisingly often the talk may turn to such themes as madness, murder, torture, syphilis, leprosy. After seeing

Chaplin with Sid Grauman, the theatre-owner and great movie-exhibitor, 1928

the painter Francis Bacon on television, he said: 'I knew at once that this was a great man. He didn't give a damn for anything or anyone! I thought, this man has such a profound

Right: Chaplin playing cricket on board the *Olympic* during his trip to Europe, 1921. Far right: posing with friends at the same period

The Japanese welcome Charlie Chaplin on his world tour of 1932. (Right: his brother Sydney and his secretary, Kono.) While they were in Tokyo the Prime Minister, Inukai, was assassinated by a militaristic secret society, the Black Dragon. It was later learnt that they had meant to kill Chaplin too

!!ンリプツヤチ !ウロハ

WELCOME FROM THE AIR
TO
MR. CHARLIE CHAPLAIN, FRIEND OF THE MODERN
PEOPLE AND A PRIDE OF THE WORLD.

This comet upon which we live is a world of comedy and pathos, and our beloved fr[iend]
Mr. Charlie Chaplain, is a living embodiment of these two fundamental elements of
worldly life.
The Clown Prince of the world today has fulfilled his ten years' desire of visiting Jap[an]
now enwrapped in the fragrant May atmosphere.
It is our earnest hope that Mr. Chaplain, who knows all the vicissitudes of life, will fin[d]
Japan more realistic and more beautiful than he has imagined her to be in his mind al[l]
these years.
I take the liberty of extending this brief, yet sincere welcome from the air to our belo-
-ved Mr. Chaplain on his arrival here today.
May 14, 1932.
DEN MIZOGUCHI,
PRESIDENT, THE MINCHO SHINPOSHA.
MINATOMACHI, KOBE.

近代人の心の友
偉大なる世界人
チャーリ・チャップリン氏
を空中より迎ふ

現代は涙と笑ひ――何れかの世界である。喜劇と悲劇
の時代相の算額を心から把握せる我等の喜劇王チ
ャーリ・チャップリン氏、日本に於けるファンの熱望
待望を茲に實現して、風薫る五月の日本を訪れ
我等はこの「甜も甘ひも知りぬいた偉大なる世界人
に對し、現實の日本が、氏の想像に生き来りし日本よ
りも真實にして美しくあるべきを確望し、このさゝや
かなる、しかし心よりの歡迎の辭を捧ぐるものである。

昭和七年五月十四日

本民社潮號機上
歡迎の辭を醉

pessimism that he can afford to be beautifully frivolous.' Chaplin – whose art has explored the narrow division between comedy and tragedy, nobility and absurdity, hope and humiliation – may have been partly referring to himself. He thinks a lot about death – especially in the form of capital punishment.

'I was pleased with the end of *Monsieur Verdoux* – the decrepit old man going off to the guillotine. When I go to the cinema now I'm always interested if there's an execution scene. Death is such a terrible thing. A living creature is such a complicated organism, it shocks me to think it can be destroyed by anything so simple as one shot, which even a child could do. You can feel the bravado and strength of an individual, with a point of view and a spirit – and then so quickly it's collapsed into a bag of useless nothing, permanently disintegrated. Somehow it's not quite so bad in a battle. I don't think I would have the courage to witness an execution – though the ceremony does have an awful drama.

'There was some clever dialogue in *Monsieur Verdoux* but now I think it was too cerebral and should have had more business. If you have a bit of a message it's better to put it over through business than through words –

better for me, anyhow. In my silent films I always used to abbreviate the sub-titles to a minimum. The best of all was in *The Gold Rush*: "Georgia! GEORGIA!! *GEORGIA*!!!" In the opening of *City Lights*, all the empty pomposity of the man's speech is suggested by meaningless noises. I used my own voice for that, with an

H. G. Wells and Gene Tunney with Chaplin at the party he gave for Wells in 1935

instrument in my mouth. And the main message of *The Great Dictator* is contained in the scene when I slide down the curtain and seize hold of the globe. By his movements, the dictator expresses all his contempt for the world.

'Nowadays, I like thinking about my favourite bits of business, but the rest is a task. They were done in moments of enthusiasm – I think all my stuff comes from being enthused. Sometimes, when I see my old films,

I think: "My God! I didn't do that, did I?" I'm surprised to think that I did it really alone. I haven't quite the same enthusiasm now. And I doubt whether the circumstances exist today to allow my sort of films to be made. As you grow older, of course, doubts come nearer to you. Life brings a certain tranquillity with it and your views change slightly. But I'm lucky, because I've got a girl who likes the same things as I like, so I'm not alone.'

I have written about Chaplin here as an old man, which is how I know him. It would have been immensely fascinating to have known him in youth and middle age – but not, I think, essential. The essence of those years has been distilled in his films: and they are a legacy to the world.

Birth of United Artists, 1919. Griffith, Pickford, Chaplin, Fairbanks and lawyers

A Chaplin Filmography

Keystone Film Company: 1914

February
1. **Making a Living** (1 reel)
Directed by Henry Lehrman.
2. **Kid Auto Races at Venice** (split-reel)
Directed by Henry Lehrman.
3. **Mabel's Strange Predicament** (1 reel)
Directed by Henry Lehrman and Mack Sennett.
With Mabel Normand and Hank Mann.
4. **Between Showers** (1 reel)
Directed by Henry Lehrman.
With Ford Sterling.

March
5. **A Film Johnnie** (1 reel)
Made under Mack Sennett's supervision.
With Virginia Kirtley and Fatty Arbuckle.
6. **Tango Tangles** (1 reel)
Made under Mack Sennett's supervision.
With Ford Sterling and Fatty Arbuckle.
7. **His Favourite Pastime** (1 reel)
Directed by George Nichols.
With Fatty Arbuckle.

8. **Cruel Cruel Love** (1 reel)
Made under Mack Sennett's supervision.
With Chester Conklin.

April
9. **The Star Boarder** (1 reel)
Made under Mack Sennett's supervision.
With Edgar Kennedy and Alice Davenport.
10. **Mabel at the Wheel** (2 reels)
Directed by Mack Sennett and Mabel Normand.
With Mabel Normand and Chester Conklin.
11. **Twenty Minutes of Love** (1 reel)
Made under Mack Sennett's supervision.
With Edgar Kennedy and Chester Conklin.
12. **Caught in a Cabaret** (2 reels)
Directed by Mabel Normand and Charles Chaplin.
Written by Charles Chaplin.

May
13. **Caught in the Rain** (1 reel)
Written and directed by Charles Chaplin.
With Alice Davenport and Mack Swain.
14. **A Busy Day** (split-reel)
Written and directed by Charles Chaplin.
With Mack Swain.

June
15. **The Fatal Mallet** (1 reel)
Directed by Charles Chaplin, Mack Sennett and Mabel Normand.
With Mabel Normand.
16. **Her Friend the Bandit** (1 reel)
Directed by Charles Chaplin and Mabel Normand.
With Mabel Normand and Charles Murray.
17. **The Knockout** (2 reels)
Made under Mack Sennett's supervision.
With Fatty Arbuckle and Edgar Kennedy.
18. **Mabel's Busy Day** (1 reel)
Directed by Charles Chaplin and Mabel Normand.
With Mabel Normand and Slim Summerville.
19. **Mabel's Married Life** (1 reel)
Directed by Charles Chaplin and Mabel Normand.
With Mabel Normand and Alice Howell.

July
20. **Laughing Gas** (1 reel)
Written and directed by Charles Chaplin.
With Mack Swain and Joseph Swickard.

August
21. **The Property Man** (1 reel)
Written and directed by Chaplin.

Chaplin performs some acrobatics during the summer of 1933 while on a fishing holiday at Catalina Island. The group on board the *Invader* (a schooner belonging to Joseph Schenck, the President of United Artists) includes, from left to right: Mrs Harry Greene, Harry Greene, Margaret Lamar and actress Paulette Goddard

This newspaper cartoon, published in 1941, was much admired by Roosevelt

With Charles Bennett.
22. **The Face on the Bar-room Floor** (1 reel)
Directed by Charles Chaplin.
23. **Recreation** (split-reel)
Written and directed by Charles Chaplin.
24. **The Masquerader** (1 reel)
Written and directed by Charles Chaplin.
With Fatty Arbuckle and Charles Murray.
25. **His New Profession** (1 reel)
Written and directed by Charles Chaplin.
With Charley Chase.

September
26. **The Rounders** (1 reel)
Written and directed by Charles Chaplin.
With Fatty Arbuckle and Minta Durfee.
27. **The New Janitor** (1 reel)
Written and directed by Chaplin.

A meeting in Paris with Josephine Baker, legendary veteran of the Folies Bergères

With Al St John.

October
28. **Those Love Pangs** (1 reel)
Written and directed by Charles Chaplin.
With Chester Conklin.
29. **Dough and Dynamite** (2 reels)
Written and directed by Charles Chaplin.
With Chester Conklin.
30. **Gentlemen of Nerve** (1 reel)
Written and directed by Charles Chaplin.
With Mabel Normand and Chester Conklin.

November
31. **His Musical Career** (1 reel)
Written and directed by Charles Chaplin.
With Mack Swain.
32. **His Trysting Place** (2 reels)
Written and directed by Charles Chaplin.
With Mabel Normand and Mack Swain.
33. **Tillie's Punctured Romance** (6 reels)
Directed by Mack Sennett.
With Marie Dressler, Mabel Normand and Mack Swain.

December
34. **Getting Acquainted** (1 reel)
Written and directed by Charles Chaplin.
With Mabel Normand.
35. **His Prehistoric Past** (2 reels)
With Mack Swain.

Essanay Company: 1915-16
(All written and directed by Chaplin. Photographed by Rollie Totheroh.)

Chaplin as guest of Chou En-lai, Chinese Prime Minister, Geneva, 1954

February 1915
1. **His New Job** (2 reels)
With Ben Turpin.
2. **His Night Out** (2 reels)
With Ben Turpin.

March 1915
3. **The Champion** (2 reels)
With Edna Purviance.
4. **In the Park** (1 reel)
With Edna Purviance.

April 1915
5. **The Jitney Elopement** (2 reels)
With Edna Purviance.

Chaplin's eldest son, Charles Jr, joined the army in 1943 at the age of eighteen

6. **The Tramp** (2 reels)
With Edna Purviance.
7. **By the Sea** (1 reel)
With Edna Purviance.

June 1915
8. **Work** (2 reels)
With Edna Purviance.

July 1915
9. **A Woman** (2 reels)

August 1915
10. **The Bank** (2 reels)
With Edna Purviance.

October 1915
11. **Shanghaied** (2 reels)
With Edna Purviance.

November 1915
12. **A Night in the Show** (2 reels)
(Chaplin plays two roles.)

December 1915
13. **Carmen** (2 reels)
(Later expanded to 4 reels by Essanay.)

March 1916
14. **Police** (2 reels)
With Edna Purviance.

Oona Chaplin hugs her daughter Josephine before the première of *Limelight* in 1952

A family party at the Manoir de Ban: Oona and Charlie with children and friends

December 1916
8. **The Rink**
With Edna Purviance and Eric Campbell.

January 1917
9. **Easy Street**
With Edna Purviance and Campbell.

April 1917
10. **The Cure**
With Edna Purviance and Campbell.

June 1917
11. **The Immigrant**
With Edna Purviance and Campbell.

October 1917
12. **The Adventurer**
With Edna Purviance, Eric Campbell and Henry Bergman.

First National Film Company: 1918-22

(All written and directed by Chaplin. Photographed by Rollie Totheroh.)

April 1918
1. **A Dog's Life** (3 reels)
Assistant director Chuck Riesner. With Edna Purviance, Henry Bergman and Sydney Chaplin.

October 1918
2. **The Bond** (split-reel)
With Edna Purviance, Albert Austin and Sydney Chaplin.
A propaganda short.
3. **Shoulder Arms** (3 reels)
With Edna Purviance and Sydney Chaplin.

June 1919
4. **Sunnyside** (3 reels)
With Edna Purviance.

December 1919
5. **A Day's Pleasure** (2 reels)
With Edna Purviance.

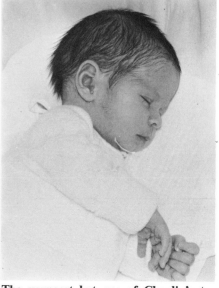

The youngest but one of Chaplin's ten children, Annette, who was born in 1960

August 1918
15. **Triple Trouble** (2 reels)
(Adapted by Essanay from a film that Chaplin had left unfinished called *Life*.)

Mutual Company: 1916-17

(All 2-reelers written and directed by Charles Chaplin and photographed by Rollie Totheroh.)

May 1916
1. **The Floorwalker**
With Edna Purviance and Eric Campbell.

June 1916
2. **The Fireman**
With Edna Purviance and Eric Campbell.

July 1916
3. **The Vagabond**
With Edna Purviance and Eric Campbell.

August 1916
4. **One a.m.**

September 1916
5. **The Count**
With Edna Purviance and Eric Campbell.

October 1916
6. **The Pawnshop**
With Edna Purviance, Henry Bergman and Eric Campbell.

November 1916
7. **Behind the Screen**
With Eric Campbell.

Christopher Chaplin, born in June 1962

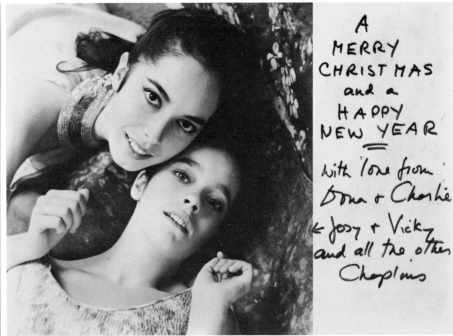

The children grow up: Josephine and Victoria, the Chaplins' second and third daughters

A MERRY
CHRISTMAS
and a
HAPPY
NEW YEAR
=
With love from
Oona + Charlie
& Josy + Vicky
and all the other
Chaplins

February 1921
6. **The Kid** (6 reels)
Assistant director Chuck Riesner.
With Jackie Coogan.

September 1921
7. **The Idle Class** (2 reels)
With Edna Purviance and Mack
Swain.

April 1922
8. **Pay Day** (2 reels)
With Phyllis Allen and Mack Swain.

February 1923
9. **The Pilgrim** (4 reels)
Assistant director Chuck Riesner.
With Edna Purviance.

United Artists Company: 1923–52
(All written and directed by Chaplin.)

October 1923
1. **A Woman of Paris** (8 reels)
Assistant director Eddie Sutherland.
With Edna Purviance and Adolphe
Menjou. Chaplin appears in a bit part,
as the station porter.

August 1925
2. **The Gold Rush** (9 reels)
Assistant directors Charles Riesner
and H. d'Abbadie d'Arrast. Photo-
graphy by Rollie Totheroh and Jack
Wilson.
With Mack Swain, Georgia Hale,
Tom Murray and Henry Bergman.

January 1928
3. **The Circus** (7 reels)
Assistant director Harry Crocker.
Photography by Rollie Totheroh.
Cameramen Jack Wilson and Mark
Marklatt. With Merna Kennedy,
Allen Garcia and Henry Bergman.

February 1931
4. **City Lights** (9 reels)
Assistant directors Harry Crocker,
Henry Bergman and Albert Austin.
Photography by Rollie Totheroh,
Gordon Pollock and Mark Marklatt.
With Virginia Cherrill, Harry Myers
and Hank Mann.

February 1936
5. **Modern Times** (9 reels)
Assistant directors Carter de Haven
and Henry Bergman.
Photography by Rollie Totheroh and
Ira Morgan.
With Paulette Goddard, Chester
Conklin, Henry Bergman and Allen
Garcia.

October 1940
The Great Dictator (126 minutes)
Assistant directors Dan James,
Wheeler Dryden and Bob Meltzer.

A Japanese poster for *Limelight*, made by Chaplin when he was in his sixties

Chaplin re-enacts one of his best known scenes: eating his boot in *The Gold Rush*

Archway Films

September 1957
A King in New York (105 minutes)
Written, produced and directed by Charles Chaplin.
Photography by Georges Perinal.
With Dawn Addams, Michael Chaplin and Maxine Audley.

Universal

March 1967
A Countess from Hong Kong (120 minutes)
Written and directed by Chaplin.
Produced by Jerome Epstein.
Assistant director Jack Causey.
Photography by Arthur Ibbetson.
With Marlon Brando, Sophia Loren, Sydney Chaplin and Margaret Rutherford. Chaplin appears in a bit part, as a ship's steward.

Photography by Karl Struss and Rollie Totheroh.
With Paulette Goddard, Jack Oakie, Reginald Gardiner, Henry Daniell and Billy Gilbert.

April 1947
7. **Monsieur Verdoux** (122 minutes)
Assistant directors Robert Florey and Wheeler Dryden.
Photography by Curt Courant, Rollie Totheroh and Wallace Chewing.
With Martha Raye, Isobel Elsom and Marilyn Nash.

October 1952
8. **Limelight** (143 minutes)
Assistant director Robert Aldrich.
Photography by Karl Struss.
With Claire Bloom, Sydney Chaplin, Buster Keaton and Nigel Bruce.

Chaplin in *The Great Dictator* (1940) which he made despite considerable opposition from the American Right, but which turned out to be a great success with the American public

3

The Early Years

I was born on 16 April 1889, at eight o'clock at night, in East Lane,
Walworth. It was still the London of Dickens. My
childhood was sad, but now I remember it with nostalgia, like a dream.
Buying lamp oil from two old ladies in a shack,
because it was a farthing cheaper. Falling into the Thames and being
rescued by a big black retriever dog. Going up to
Piccadilly where every doorway seemed to lead to something charming . . .

Ћ𝔞𝔱𝔠𝔥𝔞𝔪 𝔏𝔦𝔟𝔢𝔯𝔞𝔩 𝔊𝔩𝔲𝔟,

PORTLAND HOUSE, NEW 'CROSS *Sec., A. E. Newton.*

PROGRAM

OF

𝔙𝔞𝔯𝔦𝔢𝔱𝔶 𝔈𝔫𝔱𝔢𝔯𝔱𝔞𝔦𝔫𝔪𝔢𝔫𝔱.

For SATURDAY EVENING, *Feb. 8th,* 1896.

CHARLES DURRANT, Eccentric Comedian.

Miss CISSY LANGFORD, Serio and Dancer.

R. W. DREDGE, Male Soprano.

Miss MAUD PALMER, Serio and Dancer.

HARRY ROCHDALE, Comedian and Dancer.

Miss LILY CHAPLIN, Serio and Dancer.

WALLACE GROVES, Descriptive Vocalist.

Chairman - - - Mr. C. GHENT.
Pianist - Mr. PETER WILSON.
Stage Manager - - Mr. J. W. SPOONER.
Entertainment Secretary - Mr. J. W. LEACH.

Program 3d. *Grammer, Printer, 4, Pomeroy St., New Cross.*

My mother was a soubrette on the variety stage, with a fair complexion and violet-blue eyes. My brother Sydney and I adored her. I was hardly aware of a father and do not remember him living with us. He too was a vaudevillian (see pages 44–5) with an excellent light baritone voice. I'm very proud of my father, and a little disappointed. He was a fine artist but he drank too much. He died comparatively young, at the age of 37

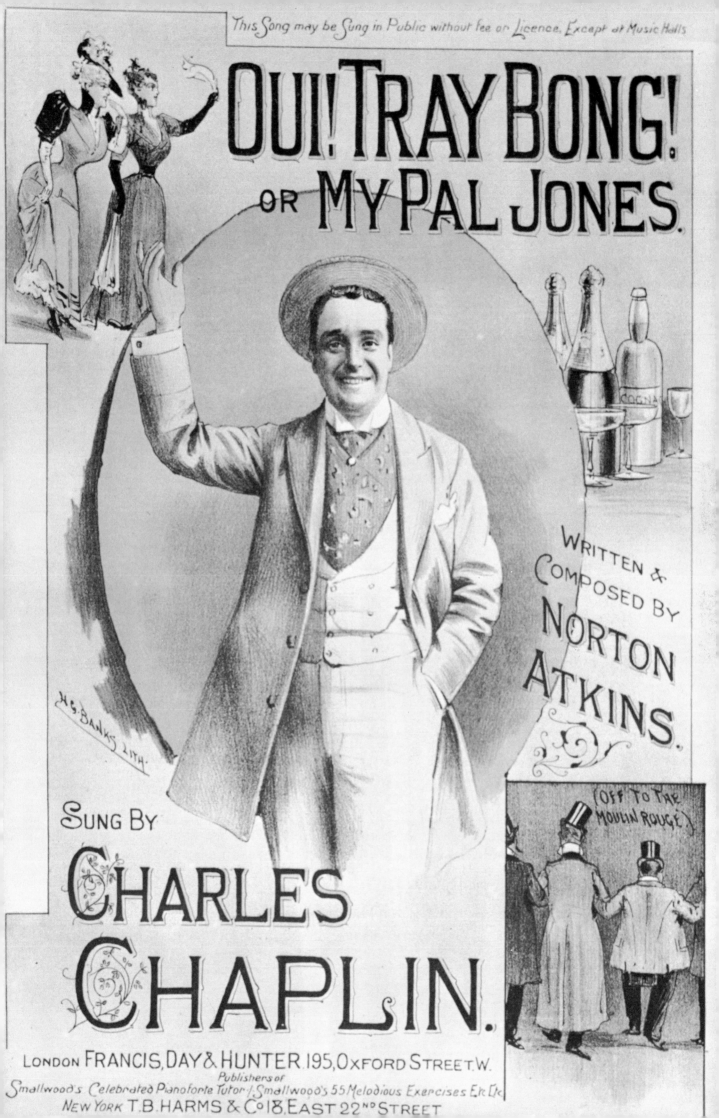

In 1896 my mother was forced to move into Lambeth Workhouse with my elder brother Sydney and myself. After th[...] half. I remember this picture being taken as if it were yesterday. I could see the camera but the camera couldn't[...]

ks we were transferred to the Hanwell Schools for Orphans and Destitute Children. Here I am, aged seven and a
I didn't realise that . I thought I was getting a full display of myself. And yet I was very unhappy during those years

The Lodge, Cuckoo Schools, Hanwell

Big picture: the Hanwell Orphanage. Above right: the Lambeth Workhouse. Above left: 287 Kennington Road, where we went in 1898 to live with my father and his mistress Louise after my mother had lost her reason and been sent to the Cane Hill lunatic asylum. The Workhouse gates are still there – one of the few places that don't let me down when I revisit these childhood scenes

When Little Charlie Chaplin Playe

Charlie Chaplin at the Age of 15. Even Today This Picture Has Features That Have Become Familiar to Millions of Movie Patrons.

Charlie Chaplin as "Billy," the Newspaper-Boy in "Sherlock Holmes," a Favorite English Stock When Chaplin Was a Lad of 14.

CHARLIE Chaplin, probably the most famous and one of the wealthiest of movie stars, has recently been revealed by a boyhood guardian as a person who always has taken his art with intense seriousness and who was bound to succeed because of his knack of making money and saving it.

This guardian, a former road-show actress, whose name is Miss Edith Scales and who now lives quietly in Scarborough, England, was moved by Chaplin's recent triumphal visit to England with his latest picture, to reminisce about the famous comedian's theatrical beginnings and some of the amusing things he did away back in 1904, when he was an ambitious young actor of fifteen.

"I first met Charlie," Miss Scales relates, "when he joined the road company which was touring England with Charles Frohman's Sherlock Holmes. There was no one to look after the boy so I took him under my wing.

"I remember one Saturday that Charlie was late for a matinee performance in which he was playing two parts, that of Billy, a newsboy detective, and of a page boy. When he finally arrived at the theatre and found that another boy was dressed in his clothes and on the stage, he broke out in tears and could not be comforted until the beginning of the second act, when he was allowed to resume his two roles.

"Even at the age of 15 Charlie was a hard-headed business man," said his onetime guardian. "To make extra money on the road he bought a five-shilling camera and during his free time, used to go about, usually amor

This newspaper article is somewhat inaccurate. I was not born in 3 Pownall (*not* Parnell) Terrace, but lived there later and on tour. I remember I was very disappointed with these pictures of Billy when they were taken. I thought th

50

As a Page Boy in the Same Play. The Bellboy Suit Is One of "Billy's" Disguises in the Action of This Thriller.

Where Charlie Chaplin Was Born—No. 3 Parnell Terrace, in Kennington Road, One of a Row of Simple English Dwellings Built in the Nineteenth Century.

of making money as beneath his dignity, even though he enjoyed the status and had the temperment of an actor.

"One day, when the company was staying at the Market Hotel, in Blackburn, Charlie noticed that the hotel sitting room was filled with farmers, in town because it was market day. He walked into the midst of the country folks and began singing songs in what was then his pronounced Cockney accent. And he finished his bit of entertainment by going into a clog dance— he was real clog dancer, too. His audience laughed until the tears streamed down their faces, but their amusement was somewhat lessened when Charlie circulated among them with his hat in his hand. He intended that his audience should pay for the impromptu show—and they did.

"Charlie wasn't mean, but he never threw away money unnecessarily. I recall how he used to check every item on the bills rendered him by landladies when we were on the road, and how he used to knock off items for service he hadn't been given. If he had been out to tea one day during the week, he would deduct a proportionate amount of the bill.

"Everybody liked Charlie, though. ___ays he was wonderfully clever. He de___

s of working people, snapping their pictures. He ___ d the photographs himself and sold them to his cus___ s for threepence and sixpence each. He was n___ to work hard, and he looked upon no honest___

___t poverty with my mother before her second mental breakdown. I played in *Sherlock Holmes* from 1901–5, in Lond___ ___remely bad. But I like them now. In 1905 I imagined myself in love with Marie Doro, who played Alice Faulkner in *Holm___

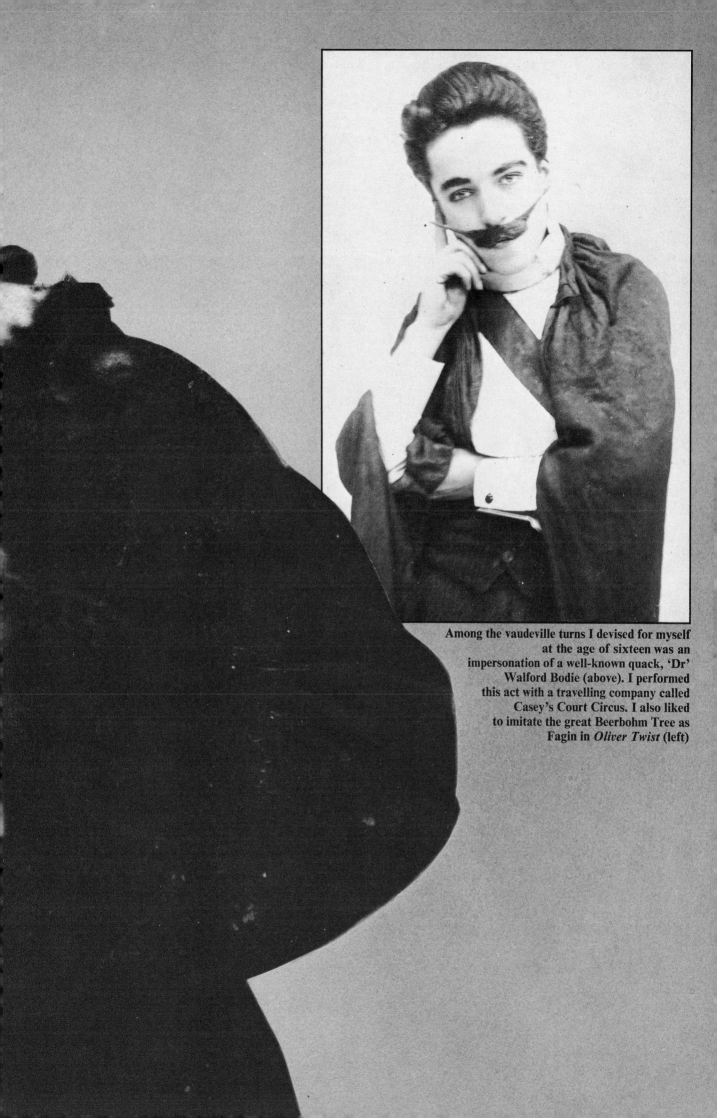

Among the vaudeville turns I devised for myself
at the age of sixteen was an
impersonation of a well-known quack, 'Dr'
Walford Bodie (above). I performed
this act with a travelling company called
Casey's Court Circus. I also liked
to imitate the great Beerbohm Tree as
Fagin in *Oliver Twist* (left)

HIPPODROME, Nottin

Direct from The NEW

CASEY'S COURT – 1906 – INC

ING THE GREAT CHARLIE CHAPLIN.

ful show but it gave me a chance to develop as a comedian. We took the name from a popular children's comic of the

l a very elaborate house that we all went to see. The actors are in front and the musicians are the ones standing behind

In 1907 Sydney (inset right, aged twenty) got me a job with Fred Karno (inset left, with his wife and a friend). My first part was in *The Football Match* at the London Coliseum. Here five of Karno's companies set off on tour from the Camberwell office.

EMPIRE THEATRE

OLDHAM.

Licensee
Mr. J. PLATT.

Manager:
Mr. ERNEST DOTTRIDGE.

PROPRIETORS:

THE OLDHAM EMPIRE THEATRE OF VARIETIES CO.
LIMITED.

TWICE NIGHTLY, at 6-50 and 9

PROGRAMME

MONDAY, MAY 3rd, 1909.

1

FRED KARNO'S
Colossal Production, entitled—THE

FOOTBALL MATCH
The Cup Tie Final.

Written by FRED KARNO and FRED KITCHEN. Music by
J. H. CLEVE. A Struggle for Supremacy between

Midnight Wanderers v. Middleton Pie-Cans
CHARACTERS BY

CHARLES CHAPLIN,
WILL POLUSKI, Junr.,

FRED NEWHAM, JAMES MANNON,
R. J HAMER, CHAS. TURNER,

Including the Professional Footballers, J. FITCHETT (late Manchester United), BILLY McOUSTRA (late Manchester City), BILLY WRAGG (Notts Forrest), JACK KIFFORD (West Bromwich Albion).
Entirely New Scenery has been specially designed, manufactured and painted by Mr. E. GRIMANI and assistants at the KARNO Scenic Factory, Camberwell.

Scene I. - - - **Training Quarters at "The Bull"**
The Middleton Pie-Cans Getting Fit.

Scene II. - - - **Exterior of the Football Ground**
The Pay Boxes—No Change Given.

Scene III. - - - - - **The Football Field**
"THE MATCH."—Stiffy in Form.

When I was nineteen I fell in love for the first time. Hetty Kelly was fifteen. I met her at the Streatham Empire where I was playing the drunk in *Mumming Birds* and she was with a song-and-dance troupe, 'Bert Coutts' Yankee-Doodle Girls'. We only met about five times. Eleven years later she wrote to me in Hollywood. She was married and living in Portman Square: would I visit her? On my way to London, I heard that she had died. This picture shows her (left) with her sister, who married the American millionaire Frank J. Gould

Arcadia Skating Rink
LEVENSHULME.

A GRAND

HOCKEY MATCH

Will be played at the above Rink

On Saturday Afternoon, April 2nd,
BULLY OFF AT 4 P.M.

ARCADIA
VERSUS
Fred Karno's Team
(From the Kings Theatre, Longsight).

FRED KARNO'S TEAM:
Goal : Ernie Stone ; Full Back : Jimmy Berrisford ;
Forwards : Fred Jordan, Ted Banks (Capt.),
and Charlie Chaplin.
Manager   -   -   Frank O'Niel.

ARCADIA TEAM:
Goal : J. Taylor ; Back : E. Stanion ;
Forwards : Birchall, Beattie, and Standfast.

S. SHUTES, Trade Union Printer, Levenshulme.

I'm sitting second from the left in Karno's
hockey team with Stan Laurel standing behind
me. Billie Reeves was one of the many fine
comedians developed by Karno in his empire of
over thirty companies. His brother Alf Reeves
the manager of Karno's American company
saw me at Birmingham in the *Skating* skit
which Sydney had written, and suggested me
for the lead in the American tour of *The
Wow-wows*. I thought this a dull, silly
sketch. Stan Laurel played my understudy in it

BILLIE REEVES.

CHARLIE CHAPLIN.

In September 1910 we embarked from
Southampton on the *Cairnrona*,
bound for Quebec. The crossing was bad,
but I only pretended to be sea-sick.
Sydney stayed in London; on his photograph
he wishes me good luck and Bon Voyage

Good Luck Charlie
Bon Voyage

ALF REEVES
PRESENTS
KARNOS
PANTOMINE CO.
IN
"A NIGHT IN A
LONDON CLUB."

The Wow-wows opened at the Colonial Theatre, New York, on 3 October 1910, and *A Night in an English Music Hall* at the Orpheum, Brooklyn, a week later. After Christmas we took them plus *A Night in a London Club* on a tour of Canada and the USA (see the scrapbook reproduced on pages 66–7 – the unnamed actor praised in the review was me!). Above: top left, Amy Minister, who married Alf Reeves (below her). Bottom left, Muriel Palmer; bottom right, Mike Asher. We returned to England at the end of 1911. Sydney had married; I took a dismal room near him in Brixton Road; I longed to return to America. In October 1912 the Karno company set sail again. The picture on the right belongs to this second American tour

"MY WORD"
But It's English
Don't You Know!

1911

MAJESTIC
Week of April 15

A NIGHT
IN AN
ENGLISH
MUSIC
HALL

20·PEOPLE·20

Six Other Big Acts
Biggest Show Yet

Where Everybody Goes

"A bloody bloomin' sparrow sat on a bloomin' spout,

When a bloody bloomin' blarsted rain

Came and washed the sparrow out!"

PANTOMIME STAR AT THE MAJESTIC

"A NIGHT IN AN ENGLISH MUSIC HALL" IS CHIEF THEME OF SHOW WEEK.

The art of pantomime is recognized in theaterdom as one of the most difficult known to the profession. It means that the actor must make known his intentions solely by signs and his general actions.

The great act known as Fred Karno's "A Night in an English Music Hall," is in considerable part pantomime and it therefore is essential that each member of the cast should be a pantomime artist of much ability.

The act shows the stage and the boxes of an English music hall. Seated in one of the music boxes is a decidedly hilarious person who evidently is suffering from too many exciting libations and consequently he insists on participating in each and every act in a manner that is so funny that the audience out in front can't help laughing enthusiastically. He scarcely says more than three words during the entire course of the act, yet so funny are his actions that he proves himself one of the best pantomime artists ever seen here.

There are many others in the cast who provide all manner of fun, and the act from start to finish is one of the greatest novelties as well as thoroughly entertaining creations ever brought to this part of the country.

Not only are various members of the cast excellent pantomime artists, but they are high class athletes and acrobats as well, for they have to take many falls and go through various stunts that only well qualified athletes could hope to successfully attempt.

The act has become the talk of Butte. Everywhere the great importation is spoken of and those who have seen it are urging their friends to see it before it concludes its Butte engagement.

Twenty people are required for its pre-

sentation and much special scenery.

The act is one of the biggest sent on tour this season and testifies to the enterprise and up-to-date methods of the Sullivan and Considine organization.

It enjoyed a remarkably long run in London and New York, and after much persuasion its proprietors agreed to send ti on tour to the northwest.

The great success with which it is meeting here doubtless will be a factor in its continued success in future.

66

ALF REEVES Presents
FRED KARNO'S LONDON COMEDIANS
In a New Pantomime Farce
"A NIGHT IN A LONDON CLUB"
or "The Amateur Entertainers"
CHARACTERS:

Archibald Binks (Inebriated).................................Chas. Chaplin
Mr. Meek (Henpecked)..Arthur Dandee
Mrs. Meek (The Pecker)......................................Muriel Palmer
Martin Harvey Dustbin (An Actor)............................Albert Williams
Percy Swoffies (A Dude).....................................S. Jefferson
Miss Taylor (A Guest).......................................Amy Minister
Agnes (The Infant Prodigy)..................................Emily Seaman
Mr. Taylor (Member of the Club).............................Mr. Asher
Mr. Clark (Member of the Club)..............................A. Austin
Mr. Jenkins (Member of the Club)............................C. Griffiths
Mr. Wilkins (Member of the Club)............................A. Seaman
Mr. Lothario (At the Piano).................................F. Westcott
The Steward of the Club.....................................Fred Palmer
The Chairman of the Club....................................Frank Melroyd
Manager for Fred. Karno's Company: Alf. Reeves. Repertoire: "Night in
London Music Hall," "Night in Slums," "Wow-Wows," etc.

INTERMISSION

First time here
"A Night in a London Secret Society"
FRED KARNO presents his Latest and Greatest Laughable Production, entitled
"THE WOW-WOWS"
In Three Scenes.   The sign of the three flaps or Pom-tiddle-om-Pom-Pompom
Written by Fred Karno and Herbert Sidney
The Cast Includes

Chas. Chaplin, as..Archibald
Arthur Dandoe, as...Charlie Blazen
Albert Williams, as...Fred Brunton
Frank Melroyd, as...Jack Denton
M. Asher, as..Jimmie Bottlie
Fred Palmer, as...Peroy
Muriel Palmer, as...Lady Binks
Amy Minister, as..Lydia Scotch
Albert Austin, Stan. Jefferson, Fred. Westcott, Geo. Seaman, etc. Supported by the Renowned Karno
Troupe of picked London performers.

Scene I. "The Nook," Depicting River Life with its beauty and gayety. PREPARE. "What man
hath joined together, let no man put asunder."
Scene II. Entrance to Secret Society's Chamber of Horrors. The password. "Kiss me. Good
Night! Nurse!" TAKE CARE.
Scene III. Interior of Chamber of Horrors. The Initiation. Archibald on the Magic Carpet
BEWARE.

Manager for Fred Karno, ALF REEVES.

I bought this coat from a musician in San Francisco on my first American tour. I thought the world of that coat. Till someon[e] said I looked like the ringmaster of a circus in it. After that I never wore it again. I can't think who 'little Mable' could hav[e] been. It wasn't Mabel Normand — I wouldn't call her 'little'! She was the pretty, dark-eyed heroine of the Keystone Comedi[es]

To little Mable
from Charlie

I took my violin to California on the Karno tour. Alf Reeves has his hat on (opposite page) and off (this page)

Above: me in downtown San Francisco. **Left:** as 'the Inebriated Swell' in *A Night in an English Music Hall*. In 1911 Mack Sennett (then an actor for D. W. Griffith's Biograph Company) saw me play this at William Morris's Music Hall in New York

The first time I was featured alone on a poster, with no mention of Karno, was at the Empress Theatre, San Francisco, in 1911. Sid Grauman, who owned the theatre, said: 'Any time you're through with the Karno outfit, come back here and we'll put on shows together.' The postcards on the right date from this period, showing me on the Mexican border, in San Francisco and in Minneapolis. I was still playing the drunk in *A Night in a London Club* two years later, this time at the Empress, Los Angeles, when Mack Sennett came backstage after the show to congratulate me. I was aware of a heavy set man with a beetling brow

Empress

MARKET ST. Bet. 5th & 6th
DIRECTION SULLIVAN & CONSIDINE

WEEK OF NOV. 5

FRED KARNO'S LONDON COMEDIANS

"A NIGHT IN A LONDON CLUB"

Empress

MARKET ST. Bet. 5th & 6th
DIRECTION SULLIVAN & CONSIDINE

WEEK OF NOV. 5

KARNO'S A NIGHT IN A LONDON CLUB

Minneapolis

He asked me casually when I would join him at the Keystone Film Company, which he had formed in 1912. I said I could start the first week in December, when my Karno contract ended. My last appearance with the troupe was on 29 November 1913 at the Empress, Kansas City. The company was returning to England and I to Los Angeles, where I would be on my own. The feeling was alarming.

The Early Films

I thought I would dress in baggy pants, big shoes, a cane
and a derby hat. I was undecided whether to look old or young, but
remembering Sennett had expected me to be a much
older man, I added a small moustache which would add age without
hiding my expression. The moment I was dressed,
the clothes and make-up made me feel the character. By the time I
walked on stage 'the Tramp' was fully born

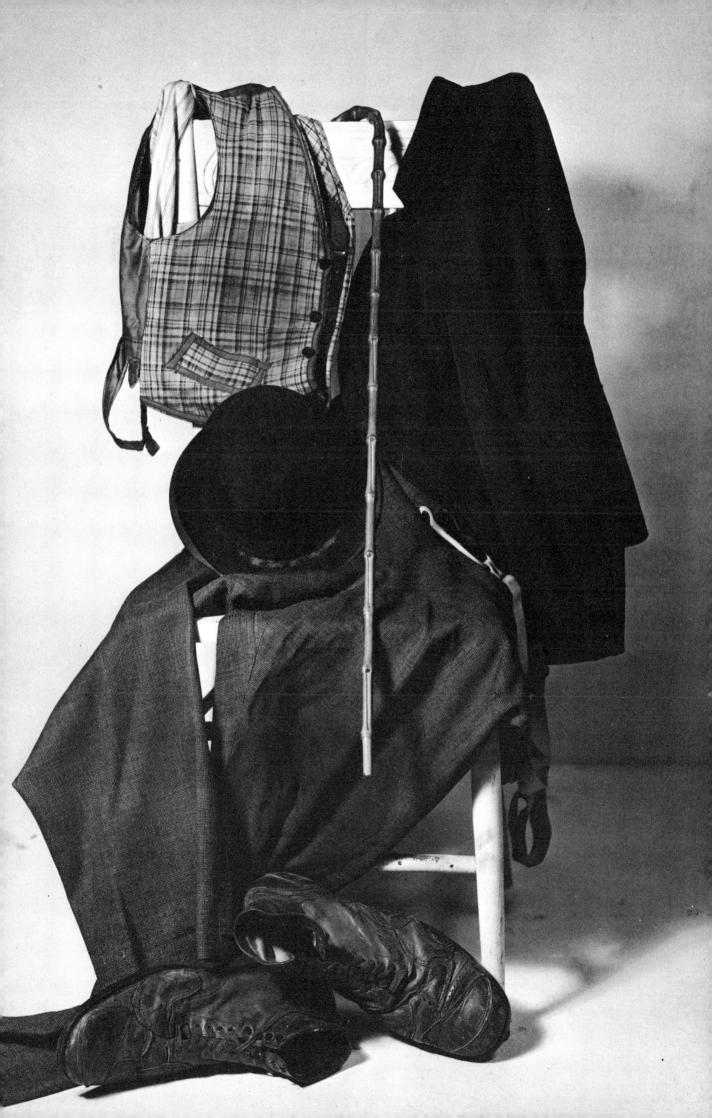

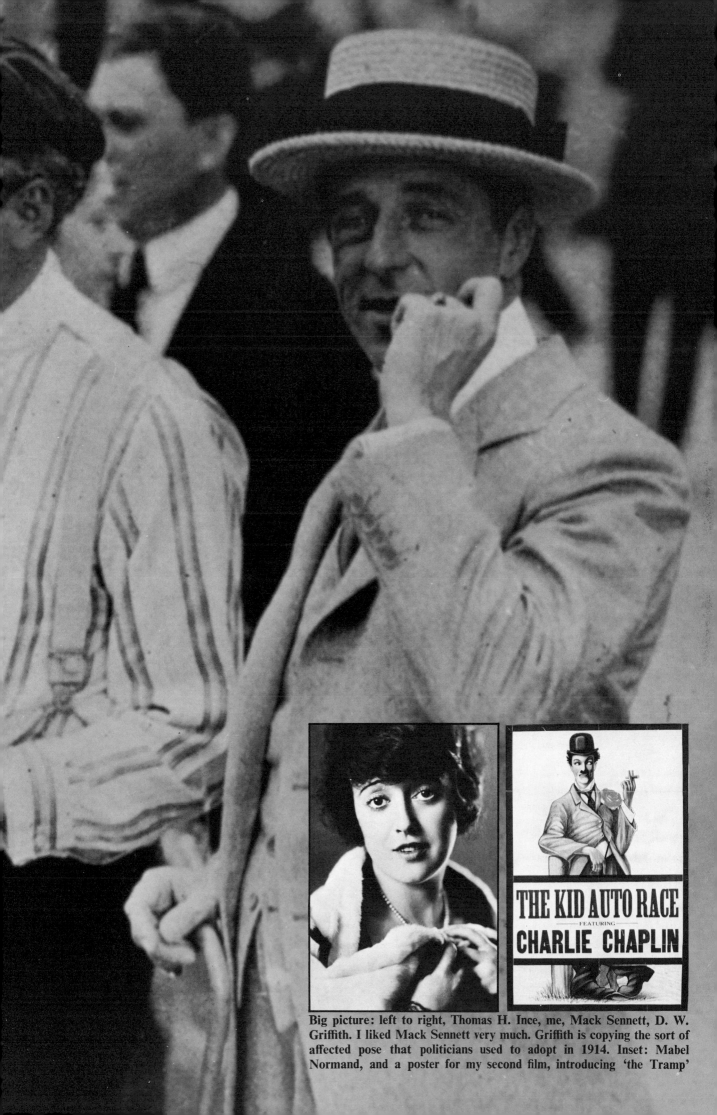

Big picture: left to right, Thomas H. Ince, me, Mack Sennett, D. W. Griffith. I liked Mack Sennett very much. Griffith is copying the sort of affected pose that politicians used to adopt in 1914. Inset: Mabel Normand, and a poster for my second film, introducing 'the Tramp'

THE KID AUTO RACE
FEATURING
CHARLIE CHAPLIN

Re-issued in 1920 as 'A Bus
The feature of Chaplin's first
This, together with the whole
a music-hall turn of Fred
referee. The film was not a

Chaplin is seeking to insinuate himself into the good graces of Minta Du
and her mother (Alice Davenpo

Chaplin's success with the ladies enrages Lehrmann and a figh.

which is tending to Chaplin's discomforture when a manservant in

nny:
hich catches every eye is the long moustache,
e, is said to date back to 'The Football Match'
; in which Chaplin was an unscrupulous
and Sennett is said to have blamed the moustache.

3

But he has a rival (Henri Lehrmann).

6

es

9

and Chaplins female escort
s, offer him consolation.

I arrived at Los Angeles and took a room in a small hotel. Next morning I boarded a street-car to the suburb of Edendale. The Keystone Studio was a dilapidated affair with a green fence round it, 150 feet square. On one set Mabel Normand was banging on a door shouting, 'Let me in!' On another was the great Ford Sterling whom I was to replace. Mack Sennett took me aside and explained their method of working. 'We have no scenario – we get an idea then follow the natural sequence of events until it leads up to a chase, which is the essence of our comedy.' I was allotted the star dressing-room used by Sennett, Sterling and Roscoe Arbuckle. For days I wandered round the studio wondering when I would start work. At last the moment came. Henry Lehrman, Keystone's top director after Sennett, was to start a new picture and wanted me to play a newspaper reporter. *Making a Living* was the first of 35 short films I made at Keystone during 1914. The pictures from here to page 99 are from a scrapbook of that period

Making a living

10

Lehrmann's profession is journalism, he is sent out in search of sensations

13

and manages in the commotion to

16

and takes refuge in a working-class ho

Chaplin creates the impression that he is heading for a career of heavy villainy tempered by acrobatics. But at intervals he brings off some happy pose or gesture giving glimpses of his future trend, as, for example, in № 12. The scenes shown represent part only of the film.

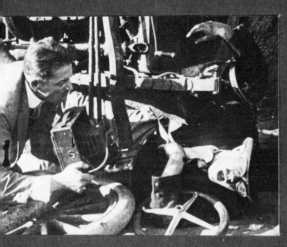 

12

lucky in being the first to ~ew a motorist who has crashed.   But Chaplin is also his professional rival

15

Lehrmann's notes and photographs. He is pursued by Lehrmann

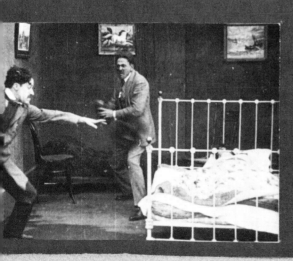 

18

~re he succeeds in locking Lehrmann into the bedroom and makes good his escape.

MABELS MARRIED LIFE

Chaplin has left his wife (Mabel Normand) alone on a bench, while he takes a stroll. On his return he finds that a gigantic stranger in sporting attire (Mack Swain) is engaging her in conversation.

He makes a dignified

undiscouraged he makes further efforts to assert himsel

The situation is saved by the arrival of Swain's wife, who scolds him an

him off.

but is met with impertinence.

only succeeds in hurting his toe.

him off.   Chaplin vents his displeasure on
           the unfortunate Mabel.

Mabel decides that she needs to study the art of self-defence,

On his return home Chaplin is confronted with the dummy and mistakes it for Swain.

Mabel plays on his delusion and flings her arms round its neck.

s a boxer's dummy to practise on

Meanwhile Swain is terrorising Chaplin in a public-house.

15

appeals in vain to its better nature.

18

in steps between them,

but a swinging blow from the dummy fells him to the ground.

THE ROUNDERS

Arbuckle returns drunk to his Hotel bedroom and   so does Chaplin.

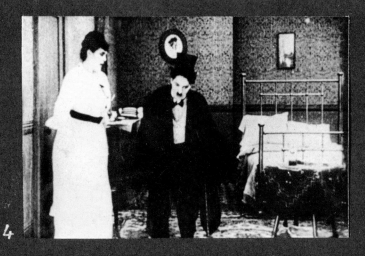

and so is Chaplin's.   The two disgraced husbands

and leave the Hotel   to visit a Restaurant.

, what a night ! '

Chaplin's balance is already precarious,

Arbuckle's wife is indignant

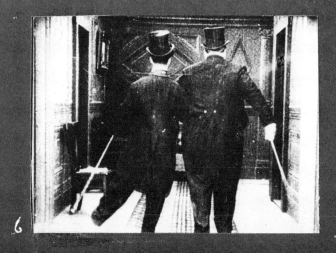

e to prolong their revelry together,

Chaplin's balance is already precarious,

The rounders

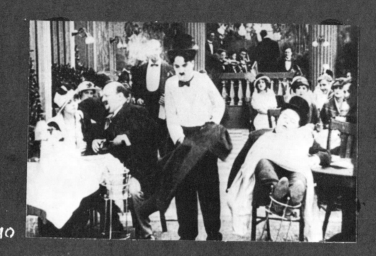

10

but they make themselves at home,

13

They hurry out of the Restaurant a

16

They board a boat which they find on

12

their wives, who have set out in pursuit, descend on them with retribution.

15

ander through a park, perilously close to the edge of an ornamental lake,

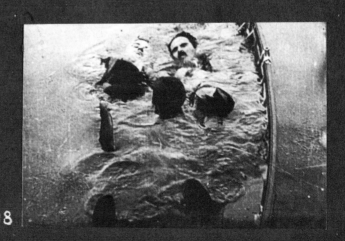

18

and settle down to sleep in it, but it sinks under them.

Chaplin tries to serve Vivian Edwards with fancy cakes but they stick to his hands, and an absent-minded gesture sends one into the ey[e]

The offended customer walks out past the proprietor (Fritz Schade) and his wife (Norma Nicholls). Chaplin hurries through to the kitchen, and falls ove[r]

and insists that Conklin aught to pick up the dishes - a fight ensues and Chaplin gets pushed down the trap-door leading to the bake-house. He ex[...]

...ue of this film was delayed until 1916.

...d in 1920 as 'Doughnut Designers'.

customer.   In attempting to repair the damage chaplin only extends it.

...her waiter (Conklin). He gets support from the Cook,

...d the ovens   and burns his fingers.

13 14

The bakehouse hands go on strike and
Chaplin is ordered to do their work.   The s

17 18

that the end sticks into   The waitresses
Conklin's eye.   and Chaplin se

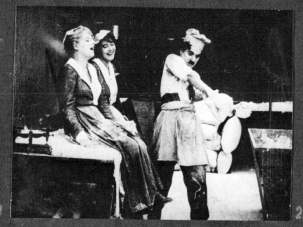

21 22

but his display of dough-kneading   Summoned to c
ends in disaster.   from the Kitche

15   16

seek to intimidate him. However he wields the shovel so vigorously

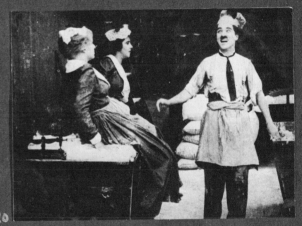

19   20

un for a chat
klin away.   He entertains them successfully for a while,

23   24

ag of flour   he charges blindly through the Restaurant with it.

Dough & dynamite

and instruct a passing child to ask that it may be put in the oven to be baked again

His attempts to carry a tray of l...

only lead to a spill. Meanwhile th...

and instruct a passing child to ask that it may be put in the oven to be baked again.

s on his head

ers insert a stick of dynamite in a loaf,

h unknowingly empties the
bin over the heads of who retaliate.
nspirators,

37   38

Chaplin demonstrates his method of making rolls

41   42

and arouse her husband's jealousy. Chaplin

45   46

likely to emerge victorious

39   40

proprietor's wife, and helps her up the ladder again.   Unfortunately his hand marks show on her back.

43   46

ack with every missile which he can find and seems

47   48

when the doctored loaf explodes in the oven.

In 1914, when Hollywood was still in embryo, Diamond Jim Brady came to Los Angeles from New York with the Dolly sisters and Owen Moore (Mary Pickford's first husband), me, Brady, Raymond Hitchcock, unknown, Sennett, two unknowns. Seated: second

...nds and gave a lavish dinner party at the Alexandria Hotel. Standing, left to right: Maurice Farquar, Lou Tellegen, unknown...
...Carlotta Monterey (later Eugene O'Neill's third wife); third from left, Mabel Normand; third from right, Edna Purvianc...

In November 1914 I signed a
contract with G. M. Anderson
(known as Bronco Billy)
and George K. Spoor of the
Essanay Company in
Chicago. I was to receive
1250 dollars a week,
and to write and direct my
films as well as act in
them. I made sixteen movies
for Essanay, most of
them featuring the beautiful
Edna Purviance (left)

The first two were *His New Job* (top)
and *His Night Out*, both two-reelers
which came out in February 1915. Edna, aged
104 nineteen, made her debut in *Night Out*

Here I am with Leo White in *The Champion*, my third film for Essanay. G. M. Anderson played a tiny part in it. It was from a combination of his initial and Spoor's that the company's title was created

I'm centre in the rather scruffy group on the postcard above, and in the photograph on top I've put on Indian headdress – no doubt as a compliment to the Essanay trademark. My first Essanay film was made in Chicago, the following five in San Francisco, and the remainder back in Los Angeles. Although the studio there was in a slummy neighbourhood, it enabled me to be near Sydney, who had replaced me at Keystone. He would finish his contract a month before the completion of mine at Essanay. My success was now so great that Sydney decided to devote his whole time to managing my affairs. I knew of my popularity in Los Angeles, but had not understood its extent

The Charlie Chaplin Book

Work (June 1915) was also known as *The Paper Hanger*, and the stove scene (left) was later included in *Triple Trouble* (1918)

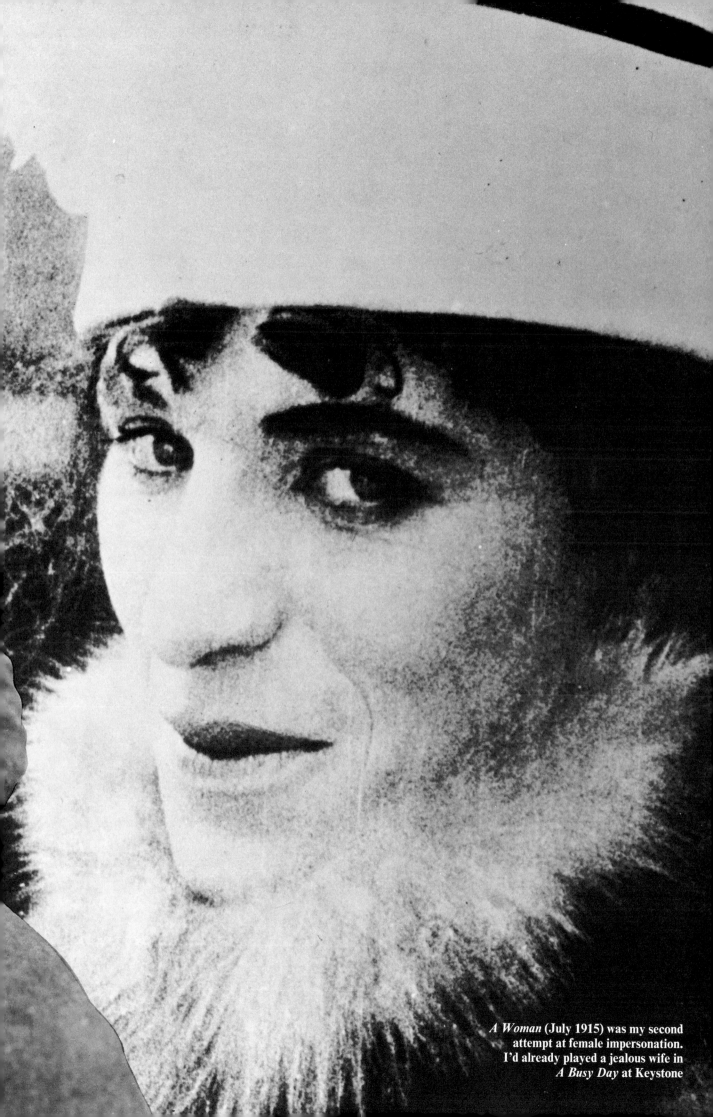

A Woman (July 1915) was my second
attempt at female impersonation.
I'd already played a jealous wife in
A Busy Day at Keystone

114   **I'm fourth from the right in the centre row at this dinner given for me in New York. I remember that the man with a moustache o**

DINNER TENDERED TO CHARLIE CHAPLIN CASTLE CAVE FEB. 10, 1916

ight – a well-known cartoonist – got drunk that night and was very funny. That's Marcus Loewe in a pointed cap in the back row   115

I wrote a lot of music at that time (I even
had my own company) and have
continued to do so ever since. I had
played the violin since I was
sixteen and once had great ambitions
to be a concert performer. As
for the cello – I could pose well with
it, but that's about all

I made my *Burlesque on Carmen* in two reels in December 1915, but Essanay added another two reels after I had left and brought it out in April 1916 much to my annoyance. This resulted in a legal battle

The Mutual Films

Early in 1916 I met Sydney in New York. He told me
he had completed a deal with the Mutual Film Company at ten thousand
dollars a week, plus a bonus of one hundred and fifty
thousand. On the evening after signing the contract I stood alone in
Times Square and watched the news flash by. 'Chaplin
signs with Mutual for six hundred and seventy thousand a year.' I read
it objectively – as if it were about somebody else

During the years 1916 and 1917
I made twelve films for Mutual, all of
them two-reelers. They were
all completed in about sixteen months
– including time off for illness

My first picture, *The Floorwalker*, was luckily a great success. It was set in a department store and included a chase on a mo

In *The Fireman* I lose the fire engine but none the less I manage to save Edna from the house which her crooked father has set alight

The Vagabond was about an impoverished violinist who rescues a beautiful gypsy girl (Edna) from a brutal gypsy chief (Cam...

One a.m. was unusual for me in that it was a solo act which took place in a very restricted space: a pure exercise in mime and tech

osity, with no plot or secondary characters. I arrive home drunk early one morning to find everything in the house against me.

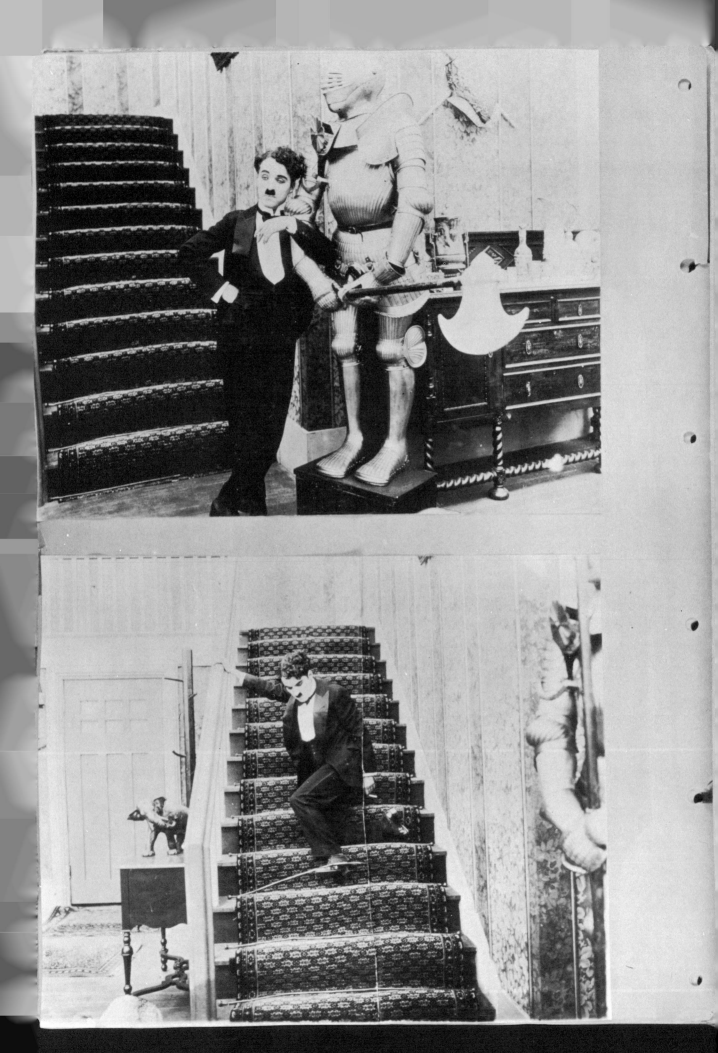

furniture, rugs, stuffed animals, staircases, doors, goldfish bowls, suits of armour, lamp-stands — all these inanimate objects con

I used to make these things up as we went along. We'd go out in the morning without an idea in our heads. In *The Count* we s

a tailor's shop with me as Campbell's assistant. I pass myself off as a Count and gatecrash a party given by Miss Moneybags.

In *The Pawnshop* I had an inventive bit of business with an alarm clock. This was the first time Henry Bergman (my boss, the pawnbr

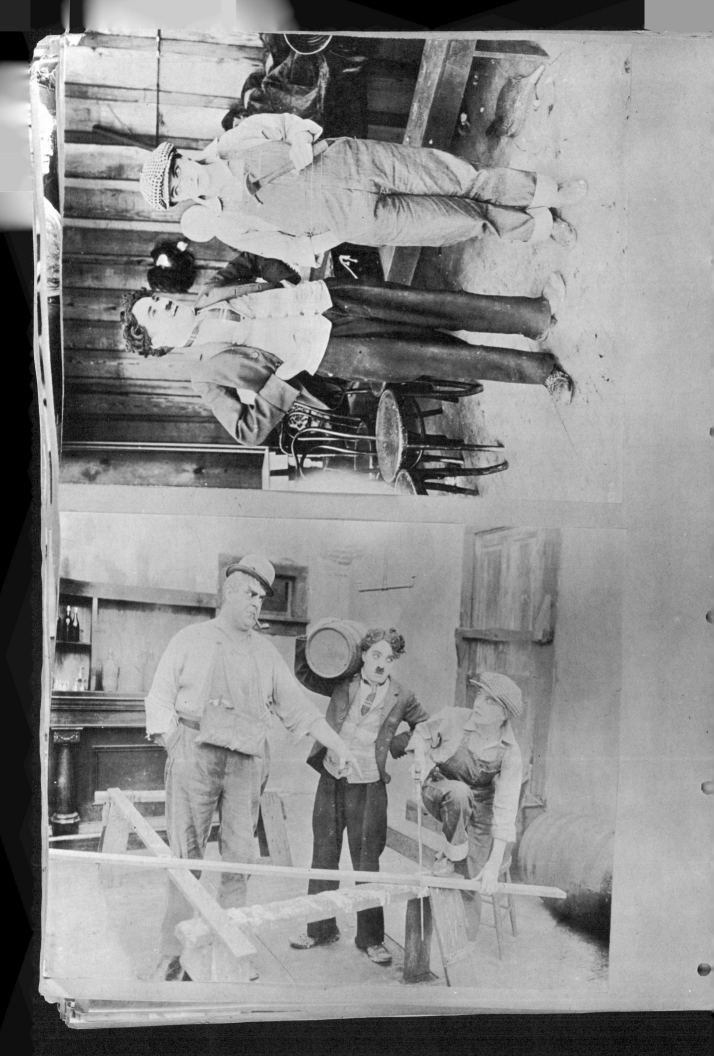

In *Behind the Screen* I'm an assistant carpenter at a film studio, Eric Campbell is my boss and Edna dresses as a boy in order to

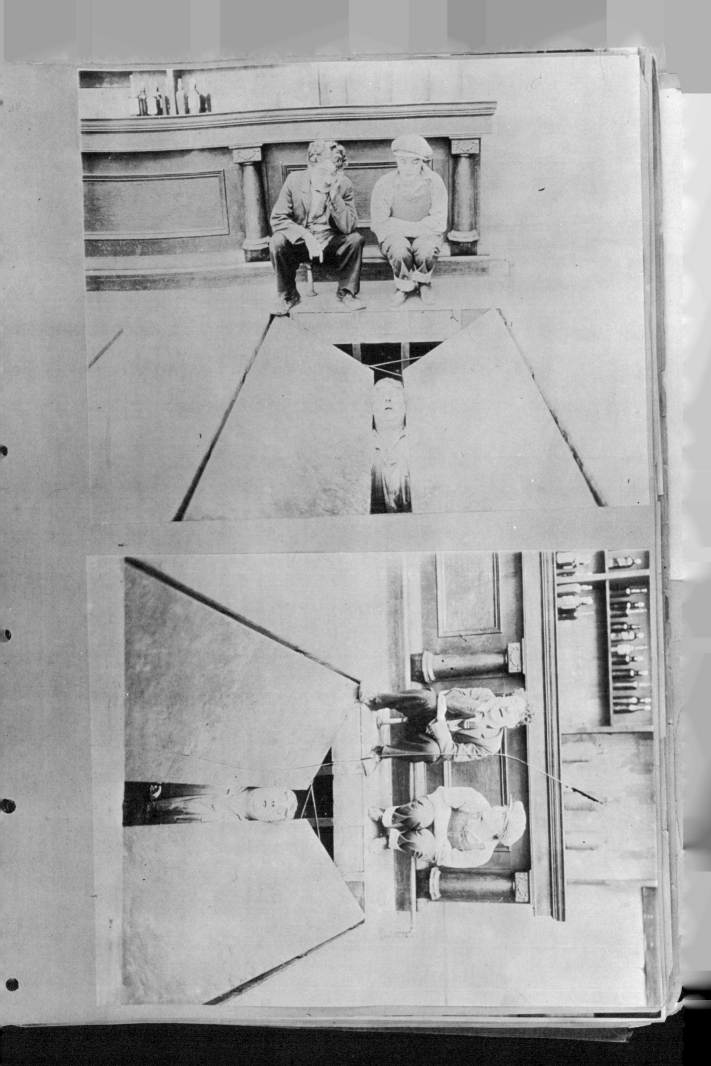

The pictures printed upside down were stuck that way in the old album from which many of these Mutual photographs are taken.

N° 2   Tous les Dimanches — 16 pages — **50** centimes   23-2-30

LES PLUS BEAUX FILMS DE CHARLOT

Patinage

A French poster for *The Rink* (left) and two scenes from *Easy Street* (above). While I was pulling the street-lamp over the big bully (Eric Campbell) to gas him, its head collapsed and the sharp metal edge fell painfully across the ridge of my nose. I enjoyed working on that old *Easy Street* set. It was based on my memories of the streets and alleys in Kennington where I spent my childhood. There's a little of that atmosphere left in London now but not much. The music to those old films was often very appropriate. I felt I had discovered music in the cinema! I always insisted on music

On the set of *Easy Street*. The cast included Edna Purviance,
Eric Campbell, Henry Bergman, Albert Austin, John Rand,
Lloyd Bacon, Frank J. Coleman, Leo White, Charlotte Mineau, Loyal
Underwood, Janet Miller Sully and James T. Kelly. Also
in the Mutual company were Leota Bryan, May White, Eva Thatcher,
Bud Jamison, Stanley Sanford, Wesley Ruggles and Tom
Wood. The camera work was by Rollie Totheroh and W. C. Foster.

I abandoned my usual tramp costume for *The Cure*
in which I take the 'water cure' at a spa
and end by impregnating the waters with alcohol

Bottom left: John Rand, Eric Campbell, Henry Bergman and me in *The Cure*. Bergman played the sadistic masseur, Rand his assis

Campbell a gouty patient. A very gentle, humble man in real life, Campbell was tragically killed in a car crash in Decemb

A first inspiring (and ironic) sight of the Statue of Liberty.
The Immigrant – with the girl (Edna) and her beautiful mother

The Immigrant touched me more than any other film I made. I thought the end had quite a poetic feeling. He carries this girl, Edna
50 her mother. Such a beautiful woman, very photogenic. I can't even remember what her name was. She just vanished and we never

My last film for Mutual was *The Adventurer* – about the hectic experiences of an escaped convict before he's recaptured. Frank J. Coleman played the guard (above)

Fulfilling the Mutual contract was the happiest period of my career. I was light and unencumbered, with fabulous prospects and a friendly, glamorous world before me

The First National Films

At the end of 1917 I joined First National, for whom I made eight films during the next five years. It was not a happy time: the company was inconsiderate, unsympathetic and short-sighted

I began building my own studio in October 1917, at the corner of Sunset Boulevard and La Brea. It was a perfect unit, with developing plant, cutting rooms and offices. Although I was so busy, I always found time for my favourite sport – deep-sea fishing

Capt.
J. Edmundson.

Weight. 162# Time 22 Min

arlin Swordfish Caught By Charlie Chaplin.
 Santa Catalina Isl. 10-6-18   Reyes

My first picture for First National was *A Dog's Life*, which I made early in 1918. I was beginning to think of comedy in a structural sense, and to become conscious of its architectural form. Each sequence implied the next sequence, all of them relating to the whole. Left: with my co-star – an excellent actor called Scraps. Top: the queue for the dole. Above: Abe Lyman's orchestra visited the set and I was allowed to conduct

DOUGLAS FAIRBANKS BOOSTING "CHARLIE" CHAPLIN TO BOOST THE LIBERTY LOAN IN FRONT OF THE SUB-TREASURY BUILDING, ALL WALL STREET LOOKING ON WITH APPROVAL. The View Is West on Wall, with Broadway and Old Trinity Church in the Distance.

MARY PICKFORD, SURROUNDED BY MEMBERS OF CONGRESS, AND WITH CHAMP CLARK, SPEAKER OF THE HOUSE, BESIDE HER. Speaking from the Steps of the United States Capitol at the Opening of the Third Liberty Loan Campaign in Washington. At Miss Pickford's Right Are "Charlie"

By 1918 America had already launched two Liberty Bond drives, and now Mary Pickford, Douglas Fairbanks and I were requested to open officially the third Liberty Bond campaign. The three of us paraded through the streets of Washington like potentates, and finally arrived at the rather rickety platform where we were to give our initial address. When I heard my name announced, I bounded on to the stage in true Fairbanksian style, and without a pause let fly a verbal machine-gun barrage in which I hardly took a breath. I spoke so vehemently and with such rapidity that I slipped off the platform and landed on top of the Assistant Secretary for the Navy – who was Franklin D. Roosevelt. Right: in this French caricature the Kaiser holds a 'special edition' of a paper called 'The Bayonet' featuring me as War Correspondent. The translated caption reads: 'Don't be jealous of Charlie, sir! Your pride need not be hurt! He will never make as many people laugh as you have made people cry!'

JALOUSIE !

Ne jalousez pas Charlot, Sire !
Votre orgueil peut se rassurer !
Jamais CHARLOT ne fera rire
Autant que vous fîtes pleurer !

My half-brother Sydney appeared as the Kaiser in a short propaganda film called *The Bond*, made late in 1918 in aid of the Fourth Liberty Bond Drive

Sincerely Yours
Sydney Chaplin

HOOVER.

Above: another scene from *The Bond*. Below: on the set with Sydney and Henry Bergman. Right: with that great artist, Sir Harry Lauder, in a similar propaganda short which we made together at the same time. This was for the benefit of the British War Loan

Charles Chaplin IN "SHOULDER ARMS" A FIRST NATIONAL ATTRACTION

With Sydney (centre) in *Shoulder Arms* (1918)

Marie Dressler came to see me while I was making
Shoulder Arms and we played the fool.
We had been friends for four years, ever since
we starred together in *Tillie's Punctured
Romance* at Keystone, which was the first feature-
length comedy film. *Shoulder Arms* took
a long time to make and I was dissatisfied with
it at first. But then Doug Fairbanks saw it
and roared with laughter – and sure enough it
turned out to be a smash hit and a great
favourite with the troops during the war. Louis
Delluc, the French critic, wrote: 'This film
justifies all that one can expect from the cinema,'
and said that I was Shakespearian!

Shoulder Arms **was made during a heat wave and working inside a camouflaged tree (as I did in one sequence) was anything but comfortable!**

A travelling troupe of midgets visited the set of *Shoulder Arms* and posed with Edna and myself.

My marriage to Mildred Harris, in October 1918, lasted under two years. Here we look like Beauty and the Beast. I hate this picture of me. I look bleary-eyed, like a murderer. No wonder!

Top left: I sign my name for use in the credits of *Sunnyside*, which was finished by June 1919. This three-reel pastoral comedy took a long time to make; it was a bit like pulling teeth. Without question, marriage to Mildred seemed to be having a very bad effect on my creative faculties

Left: a montage of scenes from *Sunnyside*.
When it was done I was at my wits'
end for an idea. Then I happened to see a
music-hall turn: an eccentric dancer
called Jack Coogan and his four-year-old
son Jackie. The little fellow had an
engaging personality. I signed him up and
gave him a small part in my next film

Form 1 (top left)

CHARLIE CHAPLIN FILM CO. — **DAILY PRODUCTION REPORT**

NUMBER OF DAYS ON PICTURE INCLUDING TO-DAY		
IDLE	WORK	TOTAL
17	4	21

DIRECTOR Charlie Chaplin - Sat - June - 14 - 1919   DATE 191
KAMERAMAN Rollie Totheroh - Jack Wilson - H.Wenger   PICTURE No. 5
WORKING TITLE Charlie's Picnic.   NUMBER OF REELS

CAST	RATE	SCENES PLAYED IN	PETTY CASH EXPENDITURES	
			ARTICLE	AMOUNT
			BALANCE ON HAND	
C.Chaplin				
Edna Purviance				
A.Austin	*			
H.Bergman	*			
T.Wilson	*			
L.Underwood	*			
T.Wood	*			
T.Boardman XG	*	5 00		
M.Feducha X	*	2 50		
R.Lee XG	*	5 00		
Bobby Kelly X	*	2 50		
Dixie Doll X	*	2 50		
K.Zimmerman T	------	------ No school today		

STILLS TAKEN TO-DAY None
NUMBER BROUGHT FORWARD None
TOTAL STILLS TO DATE None

SCENES TAKEN TO-DAY						FILM USED		STARTED WORK	
SCENE NO.	FEET	SCENE NO.	FEET	SCENE NO.	FEET	FOOTAGE		A.M.	P.M
	FORWARD		FORWARD			TO-DAY	None		
						BAL. FOTWD.	1362		
						TOTAL TO DATE	1362		

MEMO.
Did Not Shoot
Talking Story Down Town.
Children Retained

TOTAL		TOTAL		GRAND TOT.			WEATHER FAIR CLOUDY RAIN
AUTO USED			STARTED TIME		FINISHED TIME		

O.K. X - ½ day
XG - full day.   *Edward Biby*   CLERK

Form 2 (top right)

CHARLIE CHAPLIN FILM CO. — **DAILY PRODUCTION REPORT**

NUMBER OF DAYS ON PICTURE INCLUDING TO-DAY		
IDLE	WORK	TOTAL
34	9	43

DIRECTOR Charlie Chaplin - Thursday - July - 10 - 1919 DATE 191
KAMERAMAN Rollie Totheroh - Jack Wilson - H.Wenger   PICTURE No. 5
WORKING TITLE Charlie's Picnic.   NUMBER OF REELS

CAST	RATE	SCENES PLAYED IN	PETTY CASH EXPENDITURES	
			ARTICLE	AMOU
			BALANCE ON HAND	
C.Chaplin				
Edna Purviance				
A.Austin	*			
T.Wilson	*			
H.Bergman	*			
L.Underwood	*			
Tom Wood	*			
M.Feducha	*	X 2 50 ½ day		
Bobby Kelly	*	X 250 ½ day		

STILLS TAKEN TO-DAY None
NUMBER BROUGHT FORWARD 2
TOTAL STILLS TO DATE 2

SCENES TAKEN TO-DAY						FILM USED		STARTED WORK	
SCENE NO.	FEET	SCENE NO.	FEET	SCENE NO.	FEET	FOOTAGE		A.M.	P.M
	FORWARD		FORWARD			TO-DAY	None		
						BAL. FOTWD.			
						TOTAL TO DATE	6570		

MEMO.
Did Not Shoot.
Norman Spencer Chaplin,
passed on today - 4 p.m.

TOTAL		TOTAL		GRAND TOT.			WEATHER FAIR CLOUDY RAIN
AUTO USED			STARTED TIME		FINISHED TIME		

O.K.   *Edward Biby*   CLERK

Form 3 (bottom left)

CHARLIE CHAPLIN FILM CO. — **DAILY PRODUCTION REPORT**

NUMBER OF DAYS ON PICTURE INCLUDING TO-DAY		
IDLE	WORK	TOTAL
4	2	6

DIRECTOR Charlie Chaplin - Monday - Oct - 13 - 1919.   DATE 191
KAMERAMAN Rollie Totheroh - Jack Wilson - H.Wenger.   PICTURE No.
WORKING TITLE The Ford Story.   NUMBER OF REELS

CAST	RATE	SCENES PLAYED IN	PETTY CASH EXPENDITURES	
			ARTICLE	MOUNT
			BALANCE ON HAND	
C. Chaplin	* *			
Edna Purviance	* *			
A. Austin	* *			
Tom Wilson	* *			
H. Bergman	* *			
L. Underwood	* *			
A. Thalasso	* *			
C. Riesner	* *			
E. Ellsworth	* *			
Jack Coogan Jr.	* *			
M. Feducha X ½	7 50	Extra Half Day		
Babe London X ½	11 25	" "		
Jessie van Trump X ½	15 00	Finished Extra Half day		
10 Women @ 7.50	75 00	" "		
5 Men @ 7.50	37 50	" "		
4 Colored @ 7.50	30 00	" "		

STILLS TAKEN TO-DAY: 0
NUMBER BROUGHT FORWARD 0
TOTAL STILLS TO-DATE 0

SCENES TAKEN TO-DAY						FILM USED		STARTED WORK	
SCENE NO.	FEET	SCENE NO.	FEET	SCENE NO.	FEET	FOOTAGE		A.M.	P.M
	FORWARD		FORWARD			TO-DAY	2008		
						BAL. FOTWD.	10230		
						TOTAL TO DATE	18779		

MEMO.
Location: San Pedro - Boat: Ace
5.00 per hour, rented from the
San Pedro Transportation Co,
Phone: 156.

TOTAL		TOTAL		GRAND TOT.			WEATHER FAIR CLOUDY RAIN
AUTO USED			STARTED TIME		FINISHED TIME		
			A.M.	P.M.	A.M.	P.M.	

Bus - 25. per day, and
4.00 per hr, over time
day. 7.to 6
7:45 8   ② O.K. *Edward Biby.*   CLERK
Note: Bus overtime - 2 hrs

Form 4 (bottom right)

CHARLIE CHAPLIN FILM CO. — **DAILY PRODUCTION REPORT**

NUMBER OF DAYS ON PICTURE INCLUDING TO-DAY		
IDLE	WORK	TOTAL
4	8	12

DIRECTOR Charlie Chaplin - Sunday - October, 19 - 1919.   DATE 191
KAMERAMAN Rollie Totheroh - Jack Wilson - H. Wenger.   PICTURE No.
WORKING TITLE The Ford Story.   NUMBER OF REELS

CAST	RATE	SCENES PLAYED IN	PETTY CASH EXPENDITURES	
			ARTICLE	AMOUN
			BALANCE ON HAND	
C. Chaplin	* *			
Edna Purviance	* *			
A. Austin	* *			
Tom Wilson	* *			
H. Bergman	* *			
L. Underwood	* *			
A. Thalasso	* *			
C. Riesner	* *			
E. Ellsworth	* *			
Jack Coogan Jr.	* *			
M. Feducha X	7 50	Overtime		
Babe London X	11 25	" - Finished Today		
10 X Women 7½	75 00	Finished Today		
5 X Men 7½	37 50	" " "		

STILLS TAKEN TO-DAY: 0
NUMBER BROUGHT FORWARD 0
TOTAL STILLS TO-DATE 0

SCENES TAKEN TO-DAY						FILM USED		STARTED WORK	
SCENE NO.	FEET	SCENE NO.	FEET	SCENE NO.	FEET	FOOTAGE		A.M.	P.M
	FORWARD		FORWARD			TO-DAY	3493		
						BAL. FOTWD.	22288		
						TOTAL TO DATE	25781		

MEMO.
San Pedro - Boat, "The Ace"
Note: Picture Finished

TOTAL		TOTAL		GRAND TOT.			WEATHER FAIR CLOUDY RAIN
AUTO USED			STARTED TIME		FINISHED TIME		

Bus - 1 day &
Tom Wilson - clock time   9:15   O.K. *Edward Biby*   CLERK

These production sheets for the film that was finally released as *A Day's Pleasure* make interesting reading now, and give an idea of the conditions under which movies were made in those early Hollywood days. After the success of *Shoulder Arms* I had tried to get better terms from First National but had failed. I could not understand their attitude, as I was considered the biggest draw in the country. My brother Sydney explained: 'I believe it has someth[ing] to do with this motion picture convention. There are rumours t[hat] all the producing companies are merging.' Douglas Fairbanks a[nd] Mary Pickford were perturbed as well because their contra[cts] were expiring and Paramount had done nothing about it. Syd[ney] told us that we could defeat this merger if we announced to [the]

che — a. — p...a

Scene # - I - Main Title: A DAY'S PLEASURE.

"   2 TITLE # I - FAMILY Off For A Rattling Good Time.

"   3 - Med Long - Iris In * Ford At Extr of Chas Rooms - Two children enter
from door and down steps, followed by Edna and then
Chas. Children are seated by the time Chas gets down
steps - Edna also - Chas stands in fron of car. Cranks
car with his foot -

- 4 - TITLE # 2 - Everybody's Doing It.

- 5 - Continuation of # 3 - Chas starts car by cranking with hand, about to
get in as engine stops. Cranks again and starts to
get in car, engine stops. Goes back again and pulls
off coat - starts to crank but engine explodes. Starts
again to crank, but engine is going of its own accord.
A series of running back to crank.

6 - Close Up - Chas GE. BENDING OVER FRONT OF FORD - He removes overcoat, continues
cranking. Bus with optical glass and pin. Explosion -
Puts on coat again.

7 - Long Shot - EXTR WITH FORD - Repetition of racing back and forth to get in
before engine stops. Takes his place knon stops.

8 - CLOSE UP - EXTR WITH FORD - Chas gets in with car jumping. Drives out - to long

9 - LONG SHOT - Same scene - Long drive making exit, going from camera.

IO - Long Shot Back View OF Ford - Driving away with cloud of dust.

II - TITLE # 3 - THE HOLDUP AT THE CROSSROADS.

I2 - LONG SHOT - EXTR BULLOCKS STORE - Traffic cop on stand - Traffic in action -
Cop signals for street traffic to proceed - Chas enters
in his Ford - comes to cop who stops him, tells him to
get back -

I3 - TITLE # 4 - " WILL YOU KINDLY GET BACK PLEASE.?"

I4 - LONG SHOT - STORE - Chas gets back to corner -

I5 - CLOSE - STORE - CHAS & EDNA - Chas raises hat -

I6 - LONG - STORE - Cars pass Chas, he remains where he is. Gets out to crank -
Gets back in and starts to Cop - The Gossipers step
in fron of his car as he starts. Chas stops - argument.

I7 - CLOSE - STORE - GG Chas tooting his horn.

I8 - Close - GOSSIPERS - In front of Chas car.

- I9 - CLOSE - Chas tooting his horn -

- 20 - Med Close - GOSSIPERS - Underwood reclines against wheel. car backs up -
Underwood falls -

- 2I - LONG - STREET - One of the gossipers helps Undy up -

- 22 - CLOSE - GOSSIPERS ON WALK - Protesting.

- 23 - CLOSE - CHAS IN CAR-ARGUING.

- 24 - CLOSE - GOSSIPERS ON WALK - Shaking fists at Chas.

- 25 - TITLE # 5 - " STUPID ASS ! "

- 26 - CLOSE UP - GOSSIPERS ON WALK - Arguing.

- 27 - CLOSE UP - CHAS IN Car - Talking back to gossipers.

- 28 - CLOSE - GOSSIPers - Talking back.

- 29 - CLOSE,CHAS - Back talk.

- 30 - CLOSE GOSSIPERS - Back talk.

- 3I - Close CHAS - Back talk.

- 32 - CLOSE - GOSSIPERS - Back talk.

- 33 - Long Shot - Chas back on corner - He starts again just as Cop turns his
arms to stop him. He stops in center of street -
Chas is sent back as truck appears with boxes,
/////////////// /////// /////// Chas argues with cop ////
////// /// //////.

- 34 - CLOSE - TRUCK WITH BOXES & MAN IN AUTO BY SIDE OF IT -

- 35 - LONG * CHAS & COP IN CENTER OF STREET - Arguing - Chas backs up.

- 36 - MED CLOSE - Chas backs into truck with boxes - Boxes fall.

- 37 - LONG - STREET - CHas backs into truck, box falls on stout man's head -

- 38 - CLOSE - CHAUFFEUR - Removing box from man's head.

- 39 - Long - Cop turns around and goes to truck accident.

- 40 - LONG - Cop goes to accident, takes out paper and pencil - makes notes -
Stout man's car pulls out.

* 4I - LONG - COP returns to center of street. Signals for traffic to proceed -
Chas comes to cop - Cop stops him again. Men with
tar wagon come into picture.

- 42 - Close - Man dragging tar wagon - Auto backs up on tar wagon and dumps it.

- 43 - LONG - Tar all spread over ground, Chas pulls up to it and can't go further.
Fat Cop enters and goes to Ford -

- 44 - TITLE # 6 - " TAR ! "

- 45 - CLOSE p Chas in Ford p front wheels stuck in tar -

- 46 - CLOSE - Fat Cop and Tar men - Hop tells them to get it out of the way - Cop
starts to write notes - as he looks at his paper,
auto backs him into tar, in front of Chas Ford.

- 47 - LONG - FIRST COP turns and goes to Chas Ford.

- 48 - CLOSE - FAT COP - Standing in tar - Traffic cop steps to running board -
Fat cop wades out of tar and takes lid off manhole -
Traffic cop steps from running board and falls into hole.
Fat cop does not see this, and places lid back on hole.

- 49 - CLOSE FAT COP & CHAS - Chas lokks around for other cop that fell in hole.
Chas stares at Fat cop and remarks:

- 50 - TITLE # 7 - " HOW YOU HAVE CHANGED ! "

- 5I - CLOSE - HENRY & CHAS -Arguing -

- 52 - LONG - TRAFFIC COP orders Chas to get out of car - Chas pushes - Cop pushes
him into tar -

* 53 - CLOSE - FAT COP - Calling Chas to get out of tar.

- 54 - LONG - Chas & Fat Cop argue - Chas removes overcoat and throws it into his
car - Chas argues and sways back and forth.

- 55 - TITLE # 8 - " YOU'VE BEEN STICKING AROUND HERE LONG ENOUGH ! "

- 56 - LONG - CHAS & COP - Arguing - Chas drops his glove in tar - as cop stoops
forward to pick it up Chas puts out his hands and Cop falls
into the tar - Chas has both hands and feet in tar - Chas
bends over body of Cop and tries to help him up -

- 57 - CLOSE - LID OF MANHOLE - Lid comes up - Traffic Cop's head and shoulders appea

- 58 - LONG - Chas and fat Cop struggle in tar as Traffic cop emerges from hole -
Cop grabs for Chas and falls over other cop into tar -
Chas watches the cops struggle to get out - He stoops down
to remove his shoes.

- 59 - CLOSE - Chas hands removing his shoes.

- 60 - LONG - Chas climbs over the two struggling cops- paws his feet and gets into
his Ford - Leaves Cops struggling in tar - FADE OUT.

****

CHARLIE CHAPLIN FILM COMPANY
1416 LA BREA AVENUE
LOS ANGELES, CALIFORNIA

A DAYS PLEASURE - Titles

Reel # 1.

1.- The Family, off for a rattling good time.
2.- Everybody's doing it.
3.- The holdup at the cross-roads.
4.- "Will you kindly get back please?"
5.- "Stupid Ass!"
6.- Tar!
7.- "How you have changed!"
8.- "You've been sticking around here long enough."

Reel # 2

9.- All fixed up for a boat-ride.
10.- Children in arms, free.
11.- "All aboard"
12.- Three minds with but a single thought.
13.- Hamsandwitches -
Buttered Popcorn -
Cigars and cigarettes -

14.- "I'll see you later,"
15.- A forced acquaintance.
16.- The end of a perfect day
17.- The end.

---

hibitors that we were going to form our own production company
d that we intended to sell our productions on the open market
d remain independent. On the night before the convention, Doug,
ary, D. W. Griffith, W. S. Hart and myself sat at a table in the
ain dining-room of the Alexandria Hotel. Very soon half a dozen
mbers of the press were sitting at our table taking notes as we
issued our statement that we were forming an independent company
of United Artists to combat the forthcoming merger. The next da
several heads of production companies offered to resign their post
and become our president for a small salary and an interest i
the new company. After such a reaction we decided to go ahea
with our project. Thus the United Artists Corporation was forme

Jackie Coogan played the title role in *The Kid*, my first full-length film (six reels). His job is breaking windows, which I then mend. This gets us into trouble with a copper, acted by Tom Wilson (left)

An embarrassing moment arising from a mistake in identity. Phyllis Allen (the woman with the pram here) played in thirteen of my films

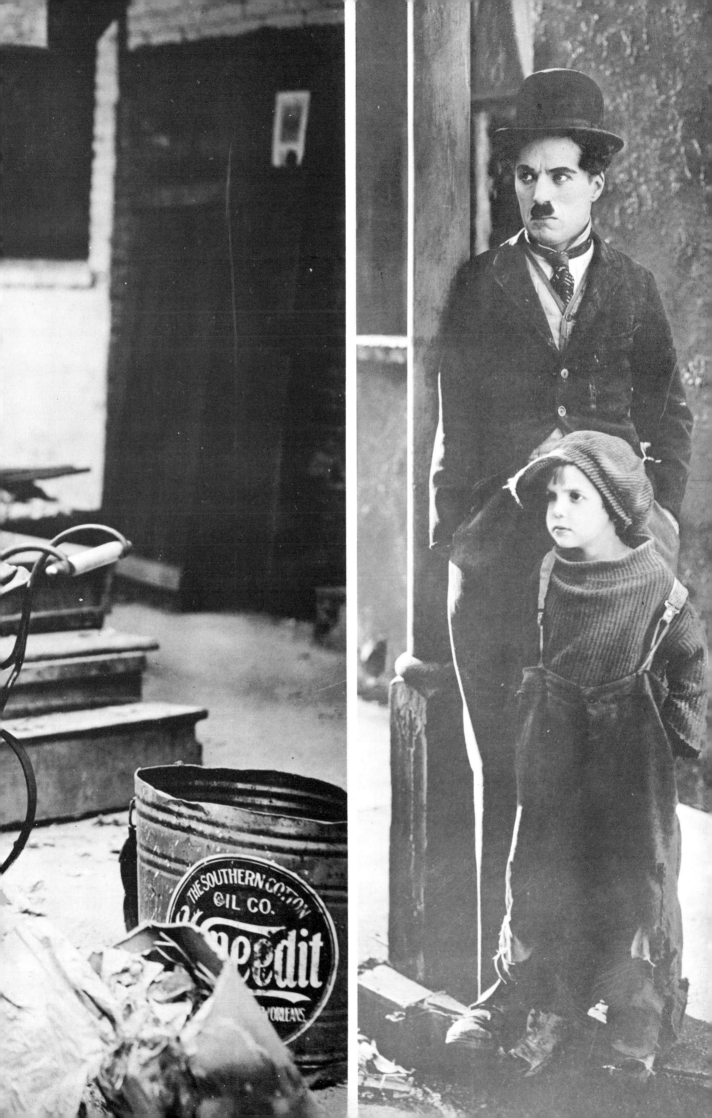

Above: other scenes from *The Kid*. Right: more visitors on the set. Coogan's father played the man who steals money from my waistcoat in the doss-house. I took the angel dream sequence bodily from Barrie's *A Kiss for Cinderella*: I told him so when I came back to London a year later. Parts of *The Kid* seem too sentimental now; fifty years makes a difference. A lot of it was shot on location in the Chinese section on the other side of the tracks, where the Los Angeles Red Light District used to be. It's all been cleaned up now. It was horribly filthy then – but it did have a certain vitality! Vitality makes up for a great deal

The main set for *The Kid* had the door centred, instead of at the side, and a sloping roof. A set means so much to me. I think myself into a thing and whatever comes out has been influenced a great deal by environment – clothes and rooms and other surroundings. This room was based to a large extent on the places in Lambeth and Kennington where Sydney and I had lived with our mother when we were children. Perhaps that's why the film had some truth. But I was never quite convinced by the part that Edna played, the mother whose desire for success is so great that she decides to abandon her own baby

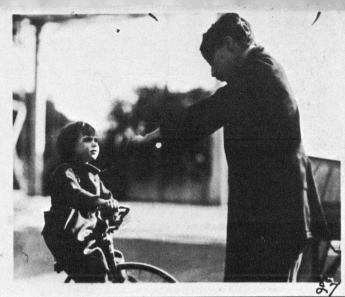

Here I'm dubiously inspecting the rushes of *The Kid*. When it eventually came out early in 1921 it was proclaimed a classic. As a result of his success Jackie made over four million dollars. I saw him again when I returned to Hollywood in 1972. A bald man with a fat tummy! It was touching

These drawings of me
were done by the
artist Fernand Léger
to illustrate a book
by Ilya Ehrenburg

Edna's maids in *The Idle Class* were played by Lillian McMurray and her daughter Lolita, who changed her name to Lita Grey and later became my second wife. After making this film, in September 1921, I set sail for England on the *Olympic* (pages 196-7)

haplin Ovation

Relaxing on the set of *Pay Day*, made early in 1922.
On pages 200–1, a montage of scenes from this film

The Pilgrim was my last picture with First National. I was a convict on the run who passes himself off as a clergyman and preaches a wild sermon. Chuck Riesner, my friend and associate director, played a crook, and his son Dinky Dean was the horrible child – an antithesis to Jackie Coogan in *The Kid*

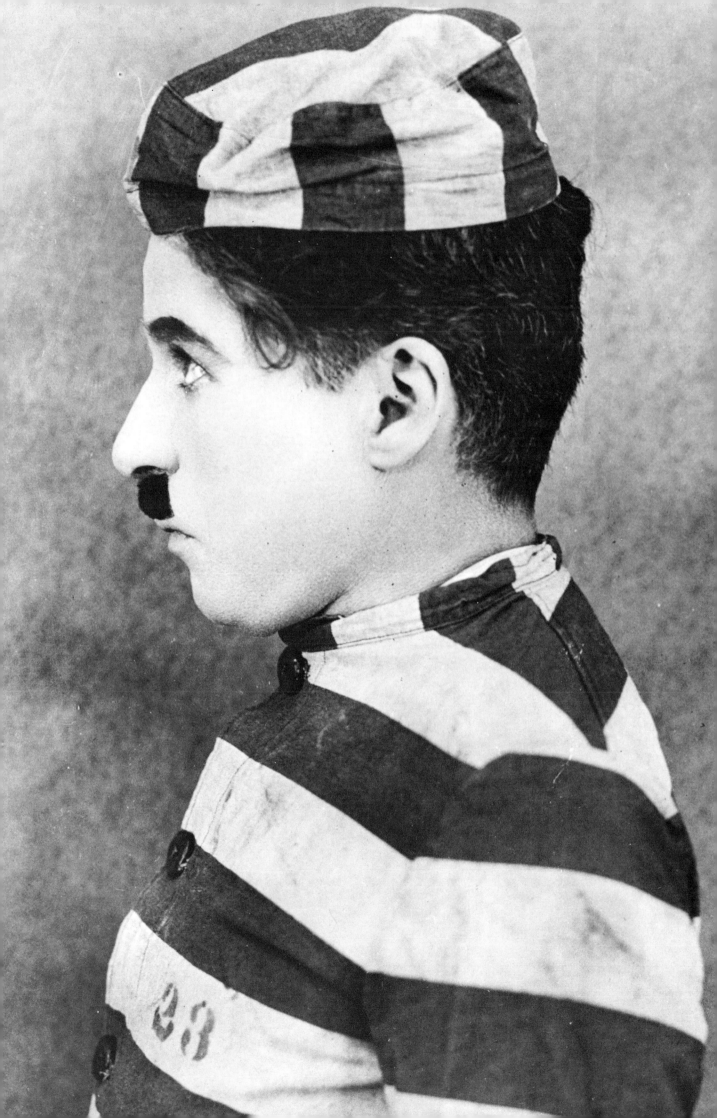

I love this photograph of Elsie Janis, the American comedienne, visiting me on the *Pilgrim* set. I was pleased to be through with First National – at last I was free to join my new associates at United Artists

The United Artists Films

Before starting on my first film for United Artists I wanted to launch
Edna in a starring role. The Empress Josephine was one
idea – and then I thought that the part of Napoleon might suit myself

My enthusiasm for Napoleon as the subject of a dramatic film subsided at last and the enterprise was abandoned. Some years later I did dress up as Buonaparte – in a comic mood this time – at a Hollywood fancy-dress party. In the top picture I'm standing next to W. R. Hearst, with Mary Pickford and Douglas Fairbanks on his right. In the lower one I'm between Marion Davies and John Gilbert, with Irving Thalberg at Marion's feet: bottom left, Eleanor Boardman; seated above her, my second wife. At that time I saw a great deal of Hearst and Marion as I enjoyed the extravagant life they led at his legendary ranch, San Simeon, and the palatial beach-house he

had given Marion. We would occasionally spe[nt] on Hearst's yacht. It was during one of thes[e] Thomas H. Ince, who had taken over Hearst's Film Productions, had to be carried off the boat He had suffered a sudden heart attack, and died o[f] three weeks later at his home. Ugly rumours be[gan] that he had been shot and that Hearst was imp[licated] not present on that trip, but I know the rumour[s were] because Hearst, Marion and I went to see Ince tw[o] his death. He was happy to see the three of us an[d] obvious that he was convinced that he would soon

There are a great many photographs of me fooling around with Doug and Mary, and we did have fun together in those days. Mary's character was rather different from her sugary image as 'America's Sweetheart', who went on playing little girls until well into maturity. She was in fact a very astute business-woman, and at the United Artists meetings I was amazed (and saddened) by her understanding of amortizations and of deferred stocks, of the legal discrepancy on page 7, paragraph A, article 27, and so on. I shall never forget her solemnly haranguing us with the phrase: 'It behoves us, gentlemen

More pictures of me and Doug. Playing billiards with us is Eddie Knoblock, my great friend – the author of the play *Kismet*. He had come with me to Europe in 1921

A Hollywood party, late 1920s.
Left to right: Gary Cooper,
Sally Eilers, me, Elsa Maxwell, the
Countess Dorothy di Frasso,
Mrs Richard Barthelmess, Mary
Pickford and Douglas Fairbanks

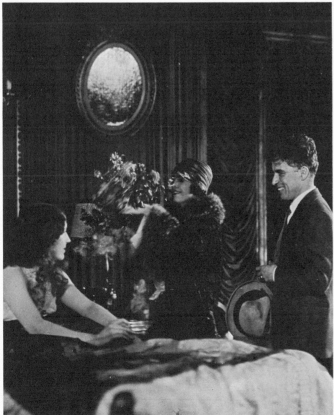

It was the celebrated matrimonial beauty Peggy Hopkins Joyce who gave me an idea for my next film. She descended on Hollywood with three million dollars collected from five husbands, wearing black for a young man who had killed himself for her, and told me several anecdotes about her association with a well-known French publisher. This inspired me to write the story *A Woman of Paris* for Edna Purviance to star in. I had no intention of appearing in the film but I directed it. Left: the central triangle – Marie de St-Clair between her childhood sweetheart, the artist Jean Millet (Carl Miller) and her rich lover, Pierre Revel (Adolphe Menjou). Above: Edna as the *demi-mondaine*; me on the set. It had a conventional plot, but I intended to express psychological subtlety by touches of irony. For example, when Marie proudly throws the necklace Pierre has given her out of the window, she then sees it being stolen by a tramp, immediately changes her mind and runs down after it. One of her heels collapses on the stairs, which adds a final touch of absurdity to her insincere heroic gesture 217

Top: among the best scenes in *A Woman of Paris* was this one, where a sardonic masseuse (Nelly Bly Baker) silently conveys her opinion of the conversation between Marie and her friend Fifi (Betty Morrissey). Above right: Jean's mother (Lydia Knott) visits Marie after he has shot himself (opposite page).

The first silent film to articulate irony and psychology, it was a great success with discriminating audiences when it came out in October 1923. It made Adolphe Menjou a star, but it failed to establish Edna. She retired from the screen soon after, but remained under contract to me till her death in 1958

CHARLIE CHAPLIN

"THE GOLD RUSH"

ABOUT THE STORY

ALASKA of the days of the Klondyke gold rush; the lone prospector; miners big and little, old and young; dance halls; dance-hall girls and hangers on; mining camp types of all sorts; assayers; ships' officers and crews; incoming and outgoing passengers; newspaper correspondents and photographers—this is the locale and these the people pictured in Charlie Chaplin's greatest of all comedies, "The Gold Rush."

Though a new note in comedy dramatics is sounded —in which the tragedies and heartbreaks of man's eternal struggle for happiness are made uproariously funny—there is, in addition, the Charlie Chaplin of old; the Chaplin of the little derby, the trick cane, the baggy trousers, the little mustache, sloppy shoes and waddling walk.

I worked on *The Gold Rush*, my first comedy for United Artists, throughout 1924 and well into 1925. I wanted it to be the greatest ever! This is an extract from a 'Press Book' of the period

Henry Waxman

Georgia Hale

She won her right to stardom by her work in "The Salvation Hunters." As soon as that picture was finished, Charles Chaplin signed her as his leading lady in "The Gold Rush," which, according to the latest reports, will be released early this summer

The feminine lead in *The Gold Rush* had been intended for Lita Grey, but after we were married I gave the part to Georgia Hale

MAY -- 1925

TARTING as an unknown in "The Salvation Hunters,"
then signed by Douglas Fairbanks, and immediately
ereafter drafted by Charles Chaplin for "The Gold
sh," is the breath-taking screen history of Georgia Hale.

Photo by Melbourne Spurr

Above: acting in *The Gold Rush*. Right: directing it. Far right: on the set with Sid Grauman, the theatre-owner, who had been on a gold rush himself in his youth and gave me advice on authenticity of detail. Tragedy and comedy are closely allied. I read a book about the Donner party who, on their way to California, missed the route and were snowbound in the mountains of the Sierra Nevada. Out of one hundred and sixty pioneers, all but eighteen died of hunger and cold. Some resorted to cannibalism, others roasted their moccasins to relieve their hunger. It was from this harrowing tragedy that I conceived one of the funniest scenes in *The Gold Rush*. In dire hunger I boil my shoe and eat it, picking the nails as though they were chicken bones, eating the laces like spaghetti. Also crazed by hunger, my partner thinks I'm a chicken he wants to eat

GR-23

The saloon in the mining town, where Charlie falls in love with Georgia, the dance-hall girl. Right: the 'dance of the rolls' – another very good gag. It just happened spontaneously, arising naturally out of the day's work. I went to the première of *The Gold Rush* in New York. From the start, with me blithely coming round a precipice unconscious of the bear following, the audience yelled. When it was over the United Artists sales manager came up and embraced me. 'Charlie, I guarantee that it will gross at least six million dollars.' And it did!

My second marriage was even more disastrous than the first. The one good that came from it was the birth of two sons – Charles Jr and Sydney (above). Lita Grey (right) had played a small part in *The Kid* before I engaged her for *The Gold Rush*. We were married in 1924 and only remained together two years. The divorce was surrounded by an atmosphere of bitterness and squalor. This period in my life was a time of great professional prosperity but also of private grief. In addition to the unpleasantness of my relations with Lita Grey, I had the deep sorrow of my mother's death. I had brought her to California when the war was over. She lived near me in a bungalow by the sea, with a married couple to run the house and a nurse to care for her. She seemed quite unimpressed by my worldly success, but her last days were happy

230 **How strange that my mother's life should end in Hollywood – seven thousand miles from Lambeth, the soil of her heartbreak! Kindness**

pathy were her great qualities. In spite of our early poverty, she had always made Sydney and me feel unique and distinguished 231

e big scene of *The Circus* is when
ave to take the place of the
ht-rope walker at the last moment
l a safety-belt enables me to
ke a spectacular start; but then I
cover it has come loose just
some monkeys who have escaped from
ir cage begin to crawl all
r my face. The film has a poetic
l touching ending, with the
cus slowly packing up and moving
, leaving me quite alone on
e deserted ground. In the first year
the 'Oscars' (1928) it won
award for 'versatility and genius'

43

Scenes from *The Circus* –
with the lion and
the clown (Henry Bergman)
and the bareback-
rider (Merna Kennedy).
I worked on this
film for two years, from
October 1925 till
October 1927. By the time
that it came out,
the talkies had been born

OLD FRIENDS ARE BACK

Mr. Battered Derby
Mr. Baggy Trousers
Mr. Bum Dogs
Miss Trick Cane
Senor Moustachio

all with

Glimpses *of Charlie Chaplin in "City Lights"*

Glimpses of
Charlie Chaplin
in "City Lights"

Charlie Chaplin in a scene from "City Lights"

Glimpses of Cha

was up against several problems. Since the advent of talkies the actors had almost forgotten how to pantomime. Their timing went into talk and not action. Another difficulty was to find a girl who could look blind without detracting from her beauty. Virginia Cherrill was beautiful and photogenic but had little acting experience. This can often be an advantage in silent films

…rawings shown on this spread were made …m artists whose handiwork appears reg-… leading papers in the most important …nd newspapers in the country. The five … shown at the bottom of the page are … drawings of Chaplin from all parts of … This is a feature which every live-wire … after for all its worth.

…or the youngsters and the thoughtfully-…re is an interesting cross-word puzzle …has been worked the name of the pic-… and the leading lady.

…miss a trick in putting over this glorious …mash. It's perhaps the biggest theatre …as ever come your way. Make it even …it is naturally, by exploiting it to a fare-…

A CROSS-WORD PUZZLE FOR THE PAPERS

Here's a great exploitation stimu- lator for use as propaganda, the giveaway and the columns of your local news- papers. It's a Charlie Chaplin "City Lights" cross word puzzle built with the name of the star and the picture worked right into the puzzle. Get your editors to run this interesting feature and offer free admissions to your the- atre for all those solving the puzzle who submit the best ten word slogans for the paper or your theatre. As it is safe to assume pretty nearly every- one in town will see "City Lights," let your free tickets be for some attrac- tion which is not likely to prove a sell-out.

With appropriate copy for an intro- duction incorporating facts about the contest carry the puzzle copy appear- ing hereunder.

ACROSS—HORIZONTAL

VERTICAL—DOWN

The cross-word puzzle is composed of the puzzle itself in two column measures and the solution in one col- umn measure. Order 17 (a) and (b). —Two Col. Puzzle Cut 50c; One Col. Solution 50c; Mat of both 10c.

Charlie Chaplin star of 'City Lights'

18—One Col. Cartoon (Mat 05c; Cut 30c)

Three years in the mak- ing for over 2 hours of fun. Charlie in his most Chaplinesque!

UNITED ARTISTS PICTURE

Charlie CHAPLIN in CITY LIGHTS

WRITTEN, DIRECTED and PRODUCED by CHARLES CHAPLIN

The laugh and the tear at a smile-a-minute pace. It's the new year's great- est screen treat!

23—Two Col. Ad (Mat 10c; Cut 50c)

Glimpses of Charlie Chaplin in 'City Lights'

29—Three Col. Cartoon (Mat 20c; Cut 75c)

ty Lights

Charlie Chaplin in a scene from 'City Lights'

31—Three Col. Sketch (Mat 20c; Cut 75c)

Charlie Chaplin
Star of "City Lights" as the cartoonists of the world see him

ARGENTINE

COSTA RICA

BRAZIL

JAPAN

SPAIN

AUSTRALIA

ROUMANIA

U.S.A.

28—Five Col. Cartoon (Mat 40c; Cut $1.25)

It is to Laugh!

The whole world rocks in agreement when it sees this convincing earthquake exploded by screendom's exalted monarch of mirth. Two years in pro- duction and a laugh for every minute it took to make.

Charlie CHAPLIN
CITY LIGHTS

21—Three Col. Ad (Mat 20c; Cut 75c)

I was determined to continue making silent films, for I believed there was room for all types of entertainment. Besides, I was a pantomimist and in that medium I was unique and, without false modesty, a master. So I continued with the production of another silent picture, *City Lights*. These pages are from a contemporary (1931) 'Press Book' for the film, which took over a year to make.

Below: *City Lights* opens with a pompous unveiling ceremony. The effect is ruined when the Tramp is discovered asleep on the statue's lap. Above left and opposite: the Tramp with the blind young flower-seller (Virginia Cherrill) whom he loves and helps

Above: trouble with the law. Pages 242–3:
my odd friendship with the unpredictable millionaire (Harry Myers) and his
supercilious butler (Allen Garcia)

I toyed with the idea of a dream sequence in which the Tramp is wealthy and distinguished, as the blind girl imagines him to be, but then I abandoned it

A joke on the *City Lights* set: I pretend to be asleep surrounded by the girls who appear in the party scene

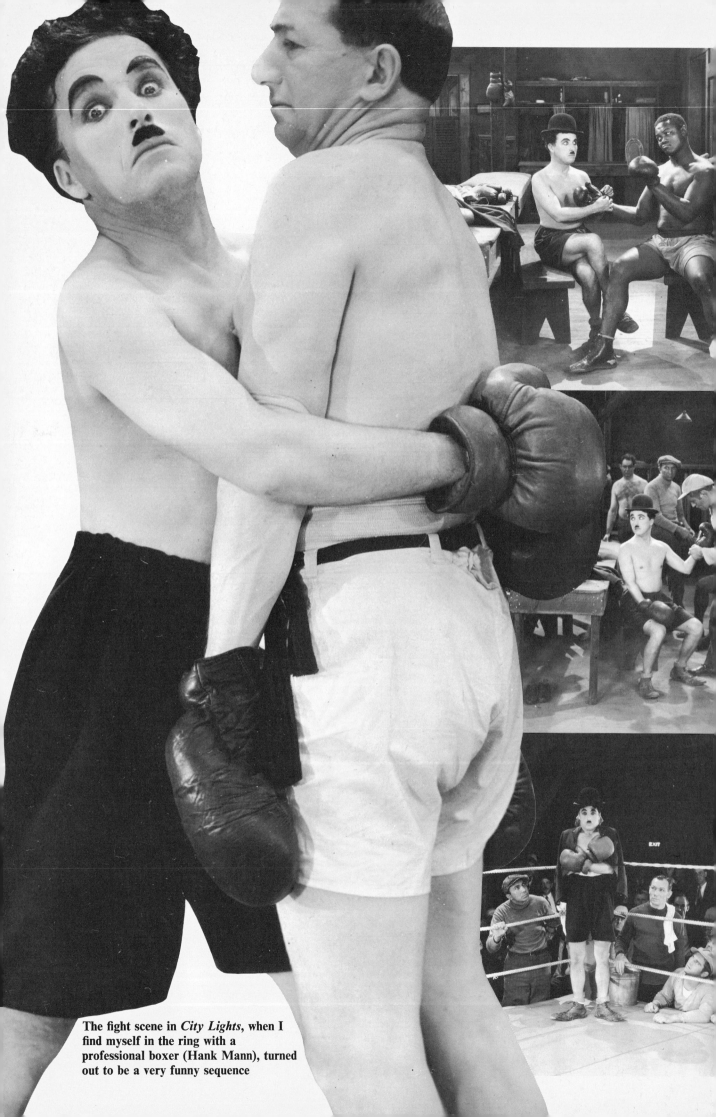

The fight scene in *City Lights*, when I
find myself in the ring with a
professional boxer (Hank Mann), turned
out to be a very funny sequence

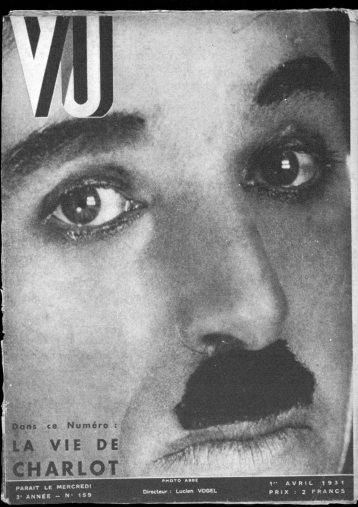

VU

Dans ce Numéro :
LA VIE DE
CHARLOT

PARAIT LE MERCREDI   PHOTO ABBÉ   1ᵉʳ AVRIL 1931
3ᵉ ANNÉE — Nᵒ 159   Directeur : Lucien VOGEL   PRIX : 2 FRANCS

The photograph on the left was taken by Edward Steichen in 1931, and the other two, from the covers of French film magazines, date from the same period. I had been worried about *City Lights*: would the public accept a silent picture? I went to the first night in Los Angeles with Albert Einstein and his wife. The audience laughed for three reels – and then the manager suddenly interrupted the screening in order to extol the beauties of his new theatre! I went mad with fury. It took a reel before they began to laugh again. Then, during the last scene, I noticed Einstein wiping his eyes. My worries were unnecessary; it was a hit with critics and public alike 249

I twice visited Tokyo – during a world tour in 1931-2, and four years later. During this second trip, Thibaud the violinist and I posed in a tea-house as two matadors trying to kill the bull – who was Paulette Goddard. Two of the most beautiful geishas in Japan looked on. Before returning to Hollywood from the holiday, Paulette and I were married

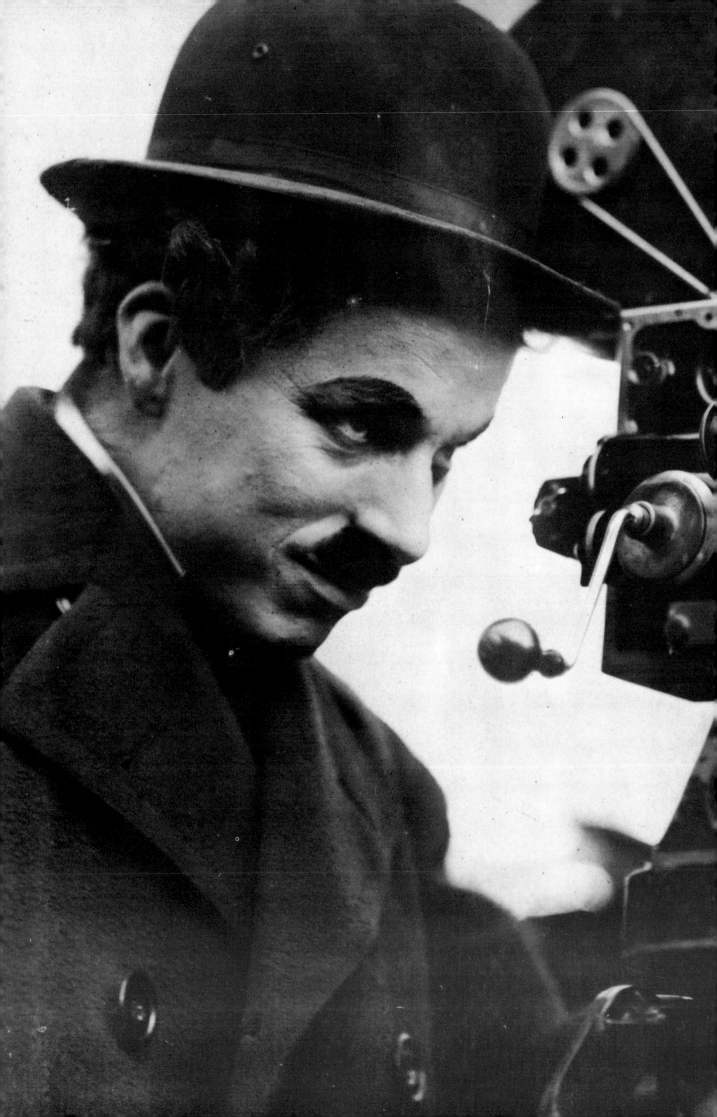

CHAPLIN SET TO RISK MILLION ON PAULETTE

Hollywood, June 7 (AP).—Charlie Chaplin is ready to risk a fortune on the gamble that Paulette Goddard can become a great motion picture star.

He said his lovely, dark-haired companion would be starred in the

Paulette Goddard
Headed toward stardom.

next picture that bears his name. He will direct and produce it but will not appear in it.

Considers Her Unique.

Chaplin considers his protegee "absolutely unique" as a screen personality.

"There's no one else like her in pictures," he said. "That, in itself, lends momentum to her debut as a star. I know she can act, she is quick to learn ——." The sensitive Chaplin hands gestured to signify his confidence.

They refused to say whether they are married.

So Hollywood has the option of interpreting his act as a fond husband's gesture toward a beautiful wife, or as the urge of one artist to bring fulfillment to another.

The Unpredictable Answer.

Chaplin doesn't care what Hollywood thinks. All that concerns him is the unpredictable answer to the question: "Will the movie public accept her as a star?"

It will cost a million dollars to find out.

Bettina Bedwell's daily fashion feature gives you the very latest in dresses, wraps, hats and all feminine accessories.

When I first met Paulette she struck me as something of a *gamine* and I thought that would be a wonderful quality for me to get on the screen. I could imagine us meeting in a crowded patrol wagon, the Tramp and this *gamine*, and the Tramp being very gallant and offering her his seat. This was a basis for several gags in my next film, *Modern Times*

It is easy to dress an actress attractively in fashionable clothes, but Paulette's outfit in *Modern Times*, like the flower-seller's in *City Lights*, needed much thought and finesse. If a *gamine* costume is treated without care, the patches seem theatrical. It was very difficult to persuade Paulette to accept smuts on her nose to make her look convincingly dirty. I had to tell her that they were beauty spots

On the set of *Modern Times*, looking as
if I hadn't an idea in my head. In
those days I was so preoccupied that I never
noticed the photographers. Probably I
was thinking about an interview I once had
with a bright young reporter on the
New York World. Hearing that I was visiting
Detroit, he told me of the factory-
belt system there – a harrowing story of
big industry luring healthy young
men off the farms, who, after four or five
years of the system, became nervous
wrecks. It was that conversation which
gave me the idea for *Modern Times*.
The factory episode (see pages 262-3)
ended with the Tramp going crazy.
From then on the plot developed out of the
natural sequence of events, through
the Depression, strikes, riots, unemployment

I had the idea of the feeding-machine as far back as 1916. In *Modern Times* it is a time-saving device to keep workers busy during lunch

The bond between Paulette and me
was loneliness. She had just
arrived in Hollywood from New York
when we first met and knew
no one. It was a case of Robinson
Crusoe finding Friday for
both of us. After the success of
Modern Times she was signed
up by Paramount to make several
films. This may have partly
caused the gradual breach between us

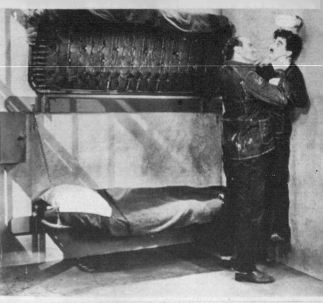

A number of scenes from *Modern Times*, including one (second from the left in the bottom row) that never appeared in the final version. Before the opening of the film on 3 February 1936 a few columnists wrote that they had heard rumours that it was Communistic in tone. I suppose this was because of a summary of the story that had appeared in the press. However, the liberal reviewers wrote that it was neither for nor against Communism and that metaphorically I had sat on the fence. These were early rumblings of a misunderstanding of my motives which grew in volume over the next decade and finally led to my departure from the United States in 1952. Of my next two films, *The Great Dictator* was openly anti-Nazi and *Monsieur Verdoux* was by implication anti-capitalist. But my troubles in this connection really started in the period after Japan had bombed Pearl Harbor and the Russians were holding off Hitler's army outside Moscow. Although Roosevelt recommended a second front, every device was used by right-wing Americans to divide us from our Russian allies. The head of the American Committee for Russian War Relief in San Francisco invited me to speak at a meeting in place of Joseph

Davies, the American Ambassador to Russia. In my speech I said: 'I am not a Communist, I am a human being, and I think I know the reactions of human beings. The Communists are no different from anyone else; whether they lose an arm or leg, they suffer as all of us do, and die as all of us die. And the Communist mother is the same as any other mother. When she receives the tragic news that her sons will not return, she weeps as other mothers weep. I don't have to be a Communist to know that. At this moment Russian mothers are doing a lot of weeping and their sons are doing a lot of dying . . .' After the meeting, John

Garfield said to me: 'You have a lot of courage.' His remark was disturbing, for I did not want to be valorous or caught up in a political *cause célèbre*. Unfortunately, he turned out to be right. Once the war was over, and the Communist witch hunts began, I was asked to testify in Washington before the famous Committee on Un-American Activities. After my appearance had been postponed three times, I sent off a telegram: 'For your convenience I will tell you what I think you want to know. I am not a Communist, neither have I joined any political party or organisation in my life. I am what you call a peace-monger

One of the trademarks of my early films had been the final fade-out, with the Tramp walking off into the distance, feet fastidiously tu

, jauntily swinging his cane. For the end of *Modern Times*, I used a slight variant. Now, for the first time, the Tramp is not alone

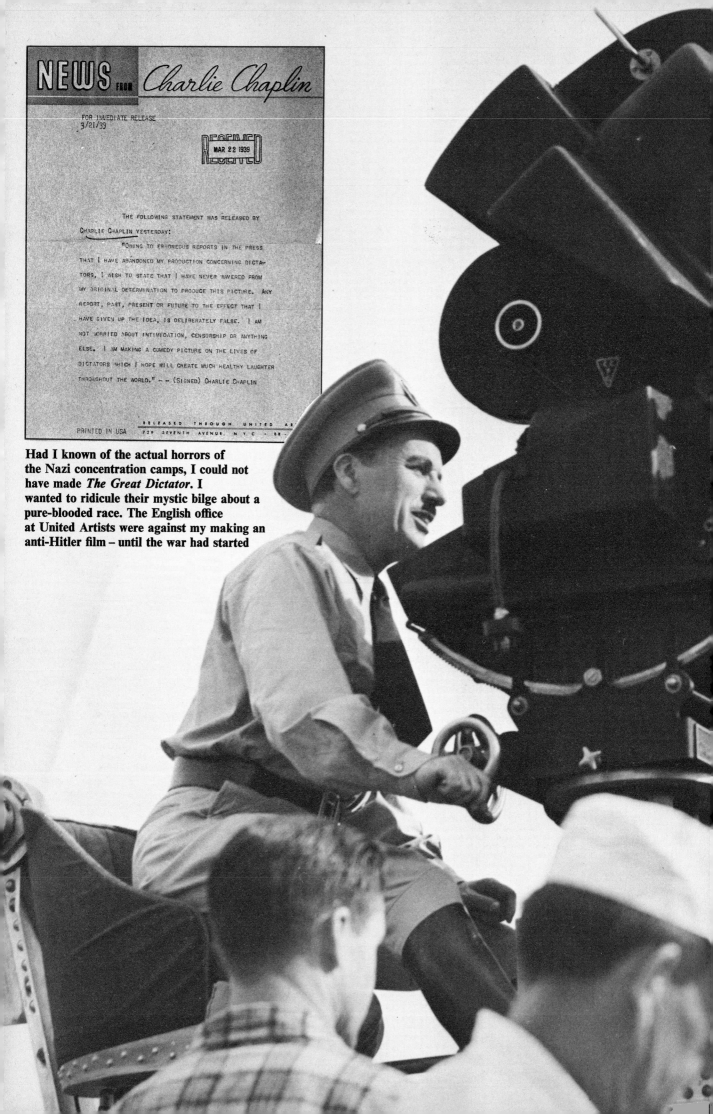

Had I known of the actual horrors of
the Nazi concentration camps, I could not
have made *The Great Dictator*. I
wanted to ridicule their mystic bilge about a
pure-blooded race. The English office
at United Artists were against my making an
anti-Hitler film – until the war had started

From left to right: Henry Daniell
as Garbitsch, Jack Oakie as Napaloni,
Dictator of Bacteria, myself as
Adenoid Hynkel, Dictator of Tomania,
and Billy Gilbert as Herring.
None of these characters in *The Great
Dictator* was quite fictitious!

In 1937 Alexander Korda had suggested I should do a Hitler story based on mistaken identity. Hitler had a moustache like the Tramp's so I could play both parts. Later it struck me that as Hitler I could harangue the crowds in jargon and as the Tramp I could remain more or less silent – ideal for my first sound film. The story took two years to develop and another year to prepare. Some of the vast crowd effects were achieved by putting Grape-nuts on a tray above a vibrator! Without such devices it would have cost five times as much. As it was, I spent five hundred thousand dollars before I began turning the camera

Opposite page: Jack Oakie in his hilarious imitation of Mussolini. This page: more scenes from the movie – including Hynkel's dance with the world, which bursts when he thinks he has it in his grasp, and the duck-shooting accident which leads to the dictator being mistaken for the little Jewish barber and vice versa

274

Studies in megalomania
– the rival dictators
try to outdo each other in
ostentatious self-display
with ludicrous results

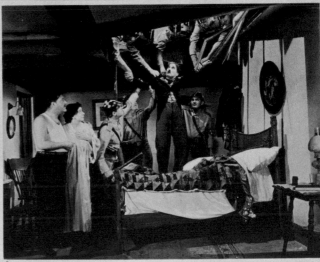

Above: scenes in the ghetto
Opposite page: Paulette
Goddard as Hannah. Left
Paulette with me. Although we
were somewhat estranged
we were still friends and remained
married until 1942. Chester
Conklin played a client of the
Jewish barber. When I had
first gone to Keystone, he had
been the only actor I was afraid
of there. He was the funniest
man in the world, I thought. He was
in seventeen of my pictures

The reviews of *The Great Dictator* were mixed. The New York *Daily News* said that I pointed a finger of Communism at the audience and most of the critics objected to the long final speech. But the public loved it and it turned out to be the biggest grosser of all my pictures up to then

Paulette and I had to push our way through the crowds outside the New York opening of *The Great Dictator* on 15 October 1940

Left: campaigning for a second front in 1942. Right: Oona, the young and beautiful daughter of the playwright Eugene O'Neill, at the time I first met her. She had been recommended for a part in my film *Shadow and Substance*. Instead of making it, I married her

Accused of violating the Mann Act, I stood trial early in 1944. Joan Barry (centre) was the chief prosecution witness. Right: my lawyer Jerry Geisler watches while my fingerprints are taken. Bottom right: during my ordeal

After the jury had deliberated for almost seven hours, I was acquitted absolutely on all counts. When my wife Oona, who was four months pregnant, heard the news on the radio at our house, she fainted

MONSIEUR VERDOUX

L'histoire d'un Barbe-Bleue moderne

Ecrit et mis en scène par
CHARLES CHAPLIN
assisté de Robert Florey et Wheeler Dryden

Musique de Charles Chaplin

★

A French publicity sheet for *Monsieur Verdoux*, **the 'comedy of murders', showing the lady-killer 'hero' with some of the ladies involved – Marilyn Nash, Martha Raye, Isobel Elsom, Margaret Hoffman and Ada-May. Miss Nash was pretty, but** – to put it politely – a little naïve. Martha Raye was very funny, though perhaps her performance was in a different key from the rest of the film. One of my assistant directors was Wheeler Dryden – who was in fact my half-brother. His father,

a well-known singer called Leo Dryden, had seduced my mother and after their son was born had taken him away to live in Canada. I shall never forget Wheeler turning up in Hollywood after I became famous and while my mother was still alive.

He made a very dramatic entrance and said: 'Do you know who I am?' To which she calmly replied: 'Of course I do. You're my son. Sit down and have a cup of tea!' I found work for him of various kinds in several of my films. He died in 195...

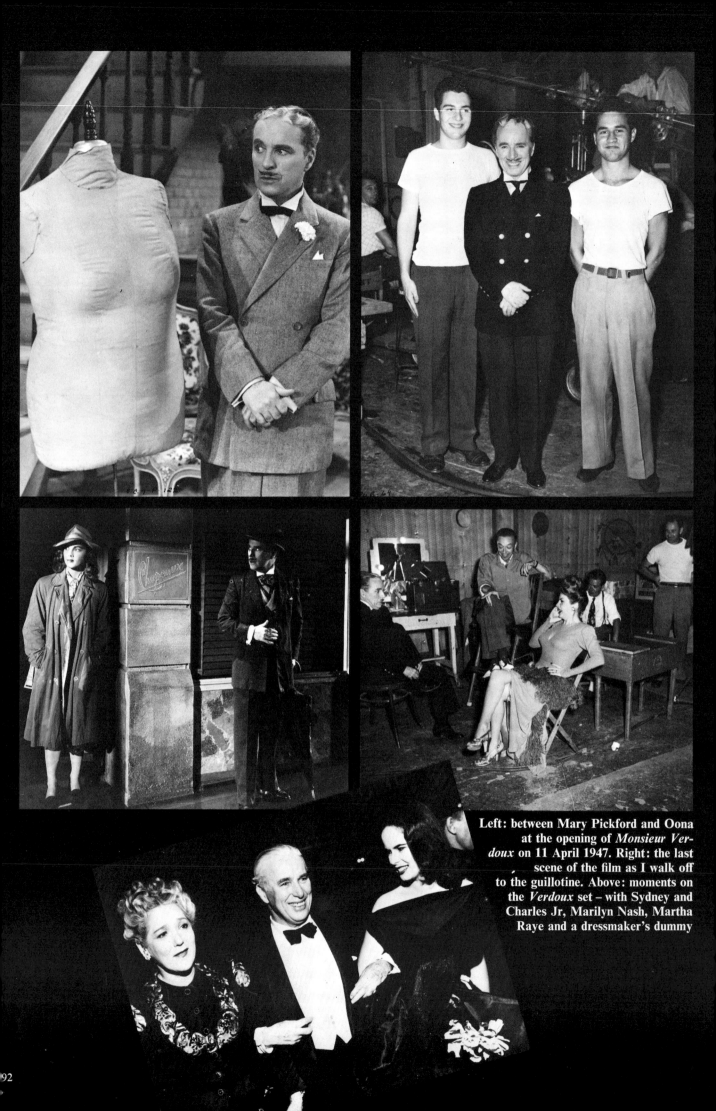

Left: between Mary Pickford and Oona at the opening of *Monsieur Verdoux* on 11 April 1947. Right: the last scene of the film as I walk off to the guillotine. Above: moments on the *Verdoux* set – with Sydney and Charles Jr, Marilyn Nash, Martha Raye and a dressmaker's dummy

Fooling around on the set of *Monsieur Verdoux* with
Martha Raye and ladies of the chorus. The
film was disliked in America where its message of anti-
materialism was mistaken for immoral cynicism

The Later Years

Since 1953 I have been living at the Manoir de Ban, Vevey, Switzerland. I was bitter at the way America had treated me, but I am blessed with a perfectly happy marriage. Oona's company makes every day an adventure and a joy. I have watched our eight children grow, composed music, written my autobiography. And I made more films. In *Limelight* (1952) I played the Great Calvero, an ageing music-hall star who has fallen on evil days

My old friend Buster Keaton appeared with me in *Limelight* as another fading comedian. 'If anyone else says it's like the old times,' he says, 'I'll jump out the window'

My children Geraldine, Josephine and Michael appeared in the beginning of *Limelight* as waifs outside Calvero's dingy home

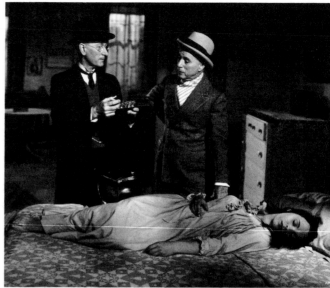

My half-brother, Wheeler Dryden, played the doctor who attends Terry (Claire Bloom) after she has attempted suicide

The character of Calvero was partly suggested by the comedian Frank Tinney whom I had seen when I first went to New York

My son Sydney played Neville, the young composer who falls in love with the dancer Terry. The film is the simple story of a ballerina and a clown, dedicated to 'the glamour of Limelight, from which age must fade as youth enters'. It was a tribute to the sentiment and melodrama of my own Victorian childhood

'That's all any of us are – amateurs. We don't live long enough to be anything else. What a sad business this is – being funny'

'We hate the sight of blood – but it's in our veins ... In the few years I have left, I must have the truth ... To live is enough'

The policeman in the ballet *The Death of Columbine* was my son Charles Jr. Wheeler Dryden also played the second clown

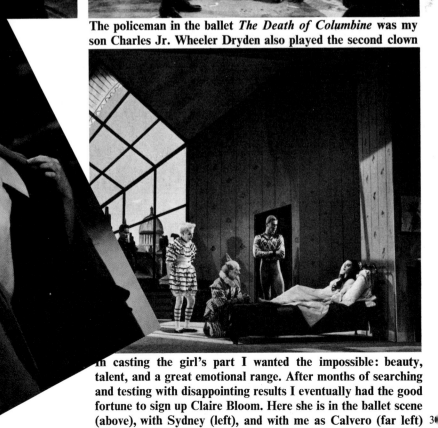

In casting the girl's part I wanted the impossible: beauty, talent, and a great emotional range. After months of searching and testing with disappointing results I eventually had the good fortune to sign up Claire Bloom. Here she is in the ballet scene (above), with Sydney (left), and with me as Calvero (far left)

My sons, Charles Jr and Sydney, were
often photographed with pretty
girls. On this page they're both with
Susan Cook and Charlie's with
Eva Kerbler. Opposite, Charlie with
Peaches Page and Syd with Joan Collins.
Charles died in 1968, aged 42

I made *A King in New York* in 1956 with Dawn Addams (below right) as my leading lady. She was very good in it – she seemed a typical American girl, although she is English. I played Shahdov, the European monarch bewildered by transatlantic civilisation

My son Michael (above) played Rupert in *A King in New York* and gave an excellent performance. But I was disappointed in the picture. I meant it to be so up-to-date and modern but perhaps I didn't quite understand it. It started out to be very good and then it got complicated and a little heavy-handed. There are some funny gags in it, like when he gets his finger stuck in the hose and it explodes in the courtroom, and when he has his face lifted and longs to laugh but daren't – yet even these seem too elaborate to me now, and I feel a little uneasy about the whole film. The critics said that it was too serious – but then I've had that complaint made about nearly all my films when they were new. They said it about *The Gold Rush* and *The Circus* and *City Lights* and *Modern Times* and *The Great Dictator* and *Monsieur Verdoux* – but later on opinions change

Family group at London Airport, 1961. Left to right: Geraldine, Eugene, Victoria, me, Oona, Annette, Josephine

ichael. Three-year-old Jane was shy and refused to pose; Christopher – the youngest – was born a year later

In 1966 I made *A Countess from Hong Kong* in London, with Sophia Loren (top), Marlon Brando (right and opposite) and Sydney (above). Oona was with me every day on the set (above right). I needed her to be there

**With Sophia Loren and Tippi Hedren at the
party on the *Countess* set for my seventy-seventh birthday**

In May 1971 I was made a Commander of the Legion of Honour at the Cannes Film Festival. And in October the following year I returned to Hollywood to receive a special Academy Award (right). I was touched by the gesture – but there was a certain irony about it somehow

In my study at Vevey, reading my latest film script, *The Freak*. It's about an angel who comes down to earth. I wrote it for my daughter Victoria (below) and we began to rehearse it – then she left home to get married. But I mean to make it one day

Acknowledgments

The author and publishers wish to express their deep gratitude to Simon d'Argols for providing coloured and back-and-white photographs for use on pages 9–13, 15–22, 24, 26 (top), 31 (centre right), 79 (bottom right), 104–5, 109, 111 (top right), 116, 119 (bottom), 140, 154 (top right), 163, 173, 180, 209 (top), 211, 224, 225 (top), 236–7, 249 (right), and 290–1.

Thanks are also due to the following for permission to reproduce photographs: Culver Pictures Inc., New York, pages 30 (top left and centre), 31 (top left), 32 (bottom), 34 (top right), 50–51, 106 (centre), 107 (centre), 108 (top left), 113, 142–3, 157, 167, 168–9, 198, 209 (bottom), 214–15, 225 (bottom left and right), 244–5, 253 (right), 268 (top left), 282–3; Raymond Mander and Joe Mitchenson Theatre Collection, pages 33 (top left), 44–5, 62–3, 220–1; The Bettmann Archive, New York, pages 32 (centre), 33 (top right), 179 (top left), 199, 207, 228 (top right), 284; Brown Brothers, Sterling, Pennsylvania, pages 33 (bottom left), 36 (bottom left); United Press International (UK) Ltd, pages 34 (centre), 35 (bottom), 36 (top left, right and bottom centre), 37 (top), 203, 286–7, 292 (bottom), 304, 305, 312–13, 314–15, 317; Penguin Photo, New York, pages 78–9, 110–11, 227 (right), 228 (bottom right), 229; Brian Love, page 103 (top); © by S.P.A.D.E.M., Paris, 1974, pages 192–3, 'Caricature of Charles Chaplin' by Fernand Léger; Mrs Steichen, page 248; Library of Congress, Washington, D.C., page 250; Cinématique Française, Paris, pages 258–9; Keystone Press Agency Ltd, pages 288–9; Associated Press Ltd, pages 302–3 and 316. All photographs not specifically acknowledged are the copyright of Charles Chaplin or the publishers.

Thanks are also due from the designer for help from Gilvrie Misstear, Red Saunders, Gugliemo Galvin and Claudine Meissner.

The publishers have made every effort to trace the owners of copyright material appearing in this book. In the event of any questions arising as to the use of such material, the publishers, while expressing regret for any error unconsciously made, will be pleased to make the necessary correction in any future edition.